OAKLAND COMMUNITY COLLEGE

3 2355 00134025 6

F
2536
.P3562

Correa da Costa

Every inch a king

Oakland Community College
Highland Lakes Library
7350 Cooley Lake Road
Union Lake, Michigan

EVERY INCH A KING

THE MACMILLAN COMPANY
NEW YORK • BOSTON • CHICAGO
DALLAS • ATLANTA • SAN FRANCISCO

MACMILLAN AND CO., LIMITED
LONDON • BOMBAY • CALCUTTA
MADRAS • MELBOURNE

THE MACMILLAN COMPANY
OF CANADA, LIMITED
TORONTO

DOM PEDRO

AT THE TIME OF THE INDEPENDENCE OF BRAZIL

Every Inch A King

A BIOGRAPHY OF DOM PEDRO I

FIRST EMPEROR OF BRAZIL

BY

SÉRGIO CORRÊA DA COSTA

Translated from the Portuguese by Samuel Putnam

NEW YORK

THE MACMILLAN COMPANY

1950

Copyright, 1950, by Sérgio Corrêa da Costa

All rights reserved—no part of this book may be reproduced in any form without permission in writing from the publisher, except by a reviewer who wishes to quote brief passages in connection with a review written for inclusion in magazine or newspaper.

First Printing

PRINTED IN THE UNITED STATES OF AMERICA

CONTENTS

BY WAY OF BACKGROUND

Brazil began as a state secret. Many years before the "official" discovery of America, Portuguese navigators and map makers knew of its existence, but this had been kept under a rigorous seal of silence in order not to awaken the ambitions of Castile, France, and England; for the secret in question was the weapon which the little Iberian kingdom counted upon by way of preserving the conquests of its bold seafarers. The Portuguese accordingly were alarmed by the voyages of Christopher Columbus and proceeded to make ready for war with the Catholic monarchs of Spain, Ferdinand and Isabella. Acting as arbiter in the dispute, Pope Alexander VI decided to imitate the example of Solomon and divide the world into two parts by means of a meridian line running one hundred leagues to the west of the Cape Verde Islands. All the westward-lying lands and seas were to belong to Spain, the eastern ones to Portugal.

The Portuguese, whose cartographers were the best in Europe, accepted the arrangement but saw to it that the line drawn by the Pope was extended 370 leagues farther west. It was in vain, meanwhile, that the French king, Francis I, protested against the pontifical decree, wittily observing that he had not seen the clause in Father Adam's will that called for a division of the universe between the rulers of the two countries mentioned. But in any event it was this imaginary line from pole to pole, cutting through the easternmost part of the South American continent, that was to constitute Brazil's first frontier, although the formal discovery of that land by Pedro Alvares Cabral did not take place until six years later, in 1500.

With barely a million inhabitants, Portugal for more than three centuries was to feel an irresistible attraction for its new dominions, those vast unpeopled spaces that were to absorb its physical and mental energies, its very lifeblood. There was, indeed, a danger that the kingdom would be depopulated as its menfolk were swallowed up in the New World so full of riches and of promise. For the criminal condemned to hard labor, Brazil meant freedom; for the bourgeois citizen, an easy means of acquiring that wealth that would put him on a footing with the *fidalgo,* or nobleman; for the tortured in spirit it offered a refuge from the implacable fires of the Inquisition; for the Jew it was the promised land; and for the mother country itself it was to come to be a reason for survival as a nation.

Conditions at home being so precarious, Brazil from an early time had to learn to defend itself by making use of its own resources in repelling the attacks of corsairs, of the French, Dutch, Spanish, and English who upon various occasions endeavored to settle along its seaboard and take possession of portions of its enormous territory. It was the Dutch that, in the seventeenth century, presented the most serious threat; for they held sway in Bahia, with a powerful fleet at their command. Yet it was during this very period of occupation by the enemy, an occupation that extended as far as Pernambuco and lasted over three decades —it was in this era that the moral unity of the country was forged, with Negroes, whites, and Indians uniting in a sacred pact to drive out the invading heretic. As the three races fought shoulder to shoulder upon the field of battle, there was sown in the blood of heroes the seed of that racial democracy that is the most striking characteristic of present-day Brazil.

At one point in the conflict Portugal itself, sorely menaced by the Castilians, was led to recognize the Dutch conquest and ordered the Brazilians to respect it; but the latter, rising as guerrillas against the Flemish, refused to lay down their arms, for they were now no longer fighting against a new ruler from abroad in favor of the old one; they were struggling to achieve their own liberty. It was the first time that Brazil had asserted itself as an independent nation.

When Napoleon decided to crush Portugal, traditional ally of the English, the Portuguese sovereign, John VI, set sail for America, along with his court and his ministers, and installed himself in Rio de Janeiro, which thereby became the capital of the kingdom. Thus by a curious process of inversion, and overnight as it were, Brazil was transformed into the seat of monarchy: it was now the mother country and Portugal the colony. For this reason it has been said that John VI, merely by setting foot upon the soil of the new land, did more for it than all his predecessors. In place of submitting as a captive to the Napoleonic despot, the house of Braganza beneath the sun of the tropics was to recover that vitality that it had lost while fettered by the contingencies of European politics. The sovereign himself, a flabby, apathetic, spineless individual, was there to feel a lost vigor flowing back into his slack limbs. Taking a deep breath, he threw off his burden of melancholy and for the first time, as he told his intimates, felt himself to be "in truth a king." Breaking with a past that had been marked by fear and submissiveness as he kept his eyes ever fixed upon the threatened frontiers of his realm, he now raised his voice and declared war upon the European tyrant; he invaded Guiana, intervened in the River Plate region, and set himself up in Montevideo, thus extending the confines of his

American dominions all the way from the Caribbean to within sight of Buenos Aires and all the way from the Atlantic to the confines of Potosí in Bolivia.

In Rio de Janeiro the court was to sink roots into the new land and draw fresh energy from the strong virgin sap which was to leave an indelible imprint upon its character. For nearly fourteen years the monarch was to struggle against political measures designed to force him to return to his age-old capital. Every form of delay and subterfuge was employed in an effort to put off this return, for the court had become American; America was now its habitat and Europe no longer anything more than a somber nightmare. Finally, with tears in his eyes, the old fellow did go back to Lisbon, in 1821; but he left behind him in Brazil the flower of the house of Braganza in the form of his eldest son, Dom Pedro, heir to the crown, and the royal grandsons, representing for him the continuity of the monarchy itself. The Braganzas, who had disembarked upon the white sands of Rio as an absolute monarchy, founded on divine right, returned to the Old World humanized, liberalized, aware of the essential rights of man. The king, once a divinity, arrived in Lisbon a crowned citizen.

In Brazil, Portugal's royal house was to evolve still further under the generous influences of the virgin land, and institutions were to spring up and flourish free of all prejudice and artificiality. When the government of Portugal, turning reactionary, later sought to deprive it of its rights and liberties, the new land gently freed itself under the leadership of a Portuguese prince; the soil on which he had grown up had nationalized him thoroughly. It was not a question of the separation of a colony, but of the splitting up of a united kingdom. For the country already, as a matter of fact, had been independent throughout the period of more than thirteen years that the court had sojourned in Rio de Janeiro. What it took the Spanish colonies long years of bloody struggle to achieve, with the result that they were broken up into a large number of small republics, Fate thus conferred upon Brazil with a free hand and so preserved its unity. While the Spaniards of the New World were still far from independence, carriages were rolling down the streets of Rio bearing ambassadors from the czar of all the Russias, the emperor of Austria, His Britannic Majesty, the king of Prussia, and other European courts.

In this manner it was that the new empire was born. And it was the young Dom Pedro, hero of the day and at once a symbol and a hope, who was to introduce a neologism into the terminology of political science: "Emperor by Acclamation of the Peoples," for such was the manner in which he was consecrated, a circumstance that caused the traditional monarchies of Europe, based upon the theological doctrine of the divine right of kings, to tremble with indignation. This book is the story of that adventurous and romantic prince. It aims to give a picture of life at the Portuguese court that had been driven to Brazil by the Napoleonic storm, and of the dawn of an American nation that holds so great a promise for tomorrow.

CHAPTER ONE

THE MAN WHO TRICKED NAPOLEON

"I cannot stand it! I cannot stand it any longer! Ah, dear Jesus! What a hell! What a living hell!"

The Portuguese court had been gloomy enough before, but tragedy now fell upon it with the piercing screams of the sovereign, Dona Maria I. Dr. Willis was sent for on the run, for it was he who had succeeded in curing the king of England of his madness. The physician's services, however, were of little avail. The queen continued to have horrible visions as devils sprang up out of every corner with glowing tridents in their hands amid a sea of flames. It was Beelzebub himself, with his hot breath, uttering eternal curses. Afterward there would be a long period of calm followed by epileptic attacks or fresh manifestations of hysteria, one fit succeeding another with painful regularity.

This saddening spectacle was due to a morbid heredity that in the case of the Portuguese royal family had been aggravated by consanguineous marriages. Daughter of Joseph I, a gouty and epileptic monarch with ulcerated legs that interfered with his lumbering gait, and the Spanish princess Mariana Victoria, who had passed on to her the mysterious nervous affection of Philip V, the unfortunate Dona Maria had not been able to escape all these degenerative stigmata. While yet a young girl

[6]

she had been given to religious delirium and prolonged spells of nostalgic depression. As heir to the throne, she had been forbidden by Portuguese law to form an alliance with a foreign prince and so had married her flabby, weak-willed uncle, who was nearly twenty years older than she.

Contrary to all expectations, their first offspring, a son, was handsome, able-bodied, and jovial, of a resolute and independent disposition, a miraculous exception in this conspiracy on the part of the forces of heredity. Rebelling against the mystical atmosphere of the court and the teaching of the friars who surrounded him, he made no effort to conceal his interest in the French Encyclopedists but kept Voltaire at his bedside, drawing inspiration from that writer's breadth of ideas, and at the same time he began a correspondence with Joseph II, emperor of Austria, the "enlightened ruler." But of a sudden he came down with the smallpox, and the queen, out of religious scruples, refused to allow the doctors to vaccinate him. The result was that he died in the prime of youth. Two months later a daughter, who had married the Spanish prince Don Gabriel and who had just given birth to a child, was likewise carried off by the disease, and the same thing happened—all in that gloomy winter of 1788—to the queen's son-in-law and her newborn grandson.

These blows, one after another, were too much for Dona Maria, who interpreted them as a sign of a curse from heaven. She must purge her own sins and those of the king, her father, who had put up with the despotism of that materialistic skeptic, the marquis of Pombal, the one who had expelled the Jesuits from the kingdom and blasphemed against our Lord. And so, more than ever, she now devoted herself to prayer, novenas, and spiritual exercises, to fastings and to penance. Then she began to hear voices and behold demons, and it was not long before these hallucinations found vent in heartrending screams and sobs. It was not until the queen had become wholly incapacitated for attending to affairs of state that the ministers and nobles of the realm turned their eyes toward the second son, Prince John, a gentle, corpulent youth who under the guidance of the friars was wholly wrapped up in the Church and its ceremonies. Melancholy and without friends, he was always to be found in the choir loft of the monastery of Mafra, intoning the plain song when he was not receiving lessons in the catechism or in Latin. Pacific-minded and a monk by inclination, all but ignored by those about him, he little suspected that he was soon to be snatched from this tranquil existence and entrusted with the direction of the vast Lusitanian Empire.

At the age of eighteen, very much against his will, he abandoned his monastic solitude for the first time in order to marry the Spanish princess Carlota Joaquina. Such marriages were in accord with traditional Portuguese diplomacy; they assured peace on the frontier, a conciliation of interests, the safety of the empire itself. Two years previously the count of Louriçal, Portuguese ambassador at Madrid, had written home: "The princess is tall, very shapely of body, all her features are quite correct, and she has very white teeth. . . ." But it was not to take Prince John long to find out how extravagant the diplomat had been in his praise. Skinny, with protruding bones and a precocious growth of down upon her upper lip, a pointed chin and large black eyes that were soon to be filled with malice—such was Dona Carlota at thirteen, the age at which the marriage was consummated. The princess's father, Charles IV, was known for his chastity and as a collector of watches. He was a man whose weakness of will stood in contrast to the might of his fists, for he frequently engaged in uproarious boxing bouts with his own lackies. Dona Carlota's mother was Italian, Maria Luisa of Parma, an ambitious woman whose fondness for command was written upon her angular face, a face dominated by her dark and sparkling eyes; it was from her that the daughter was to inherit the fits of stubbornness that she displayed together with a genius for intrigue, a natural turn for politics, and a lascivious temperament.

A hurricane had been unleashed upon the calm that Prince John once had known. It is related that when he approached his bride for a first kiss he suddenly fell back with a cry of pain, for in place of a kiss she had given him a lusty bite on the ear. And that was not all. She followed it up by striking him across the royal forehead with a heavy candlestick. How she was to change where men were concerned!

The affair became a scandal and certain verses began to go the rounds:

> Everyone is saying,
> As anyone may hear,
> That cat and tomcat had a quarrel
> And she bit him on the ear.

Despite the fact that they were never meant to understand each other, Prince John and Dona Carlota brilliantly fulfilled their reproductive functions and by 1803 had already brought eight young ones into the world. Dona Maria Teresa, the first born, saw the light in that tempestuous year 1793, just as the throne of the Bourbons was coming down with a tremendous crash. The second one was a son, Dom Antonio, heir to the throne. His birth was celebrated with pomp and rejoicing, to the pealing of bells and salvos of artillery, but he died at the age of seven. Still they continued to come: Dona Maria Isabel, destined to be the bride of Ferdinand VII of Spain; Dom Pedro, future emperor of Brazil, born in 1798; two more princesses, Maria Francisca and Isabel-Maria; Dom Miguel, in 1802; and finally, another pair of princesses, Dona Maria de Assunção and Dona Ana de

Jesús Maria, the last mentioned being born in 1806. Then the conjugal pair parted company so far as the marriage bed was concerned, and each went his own way, Dona Carlota to seek adventures while Prince John went back to the organ and his opulent repertory of Gregorian chants.

When this peacefully inclined prince was called to assume the reins of government, Europe was in a whirlwind. In Paris, under the pickaxes of an infuriated populace, the eight huge towers of the Bastille had already fallen, even as an assembly of philosophers sought to compel the world to submit to their wildly subversive doctrines. And along with the reigning dynasty the Church likewise suffered shipwreck amid the horrible sacrileges of the Black Mass. Shortly afterward Napoleon fell upon the Continent. It was chaos reaping the whirlwind. Nothing could resist the onslaught of his artillery or the mad charges of his grenadiers. Frontiers and thrones that had endured for centuries now went down before the gun butts of this adventurer who was out to conquer a world.

Small and defenseless, Portugal uneasily awaited its turn. From his gloomy country estate at Queluz, Prince John endeavored to find some means of warding off the inevitable blow. He temporized as long as he could, in every way that he could, for his preferred tactics consisted of evasion and delay. Came Trafalgar, and Napoleon was convinced that it was essential to cut off the English from the continent to which Portugal was an open door. One way or another he would close that door, and so he sent an ultimatum to the effect that the regent was to break at once with England in order that his country might join the continental blockade. To attempt to resist Franco-Spanish aggression—the Pyrenees were wide open—would have been madness. So true was this that when one of the ministers, Rodrigo de Souza Coutinho, proposed in the council of state that they make the army ready for that purpose, he met with a chorus of indignation.

"Let us not think of arming, gentlemen; we must not arouse the anger of the French!" And the minister Araujo added, with strong emphasis: "Resist? Defend ourselves? But how? We have nothing!" [1]

As for Prince John, he hesitated no longer between Napoleon and England; it was a question, rather, of choosing between Portugal and Brazil. If he set out for America, the kingdom would be gobbled up by the voracious Franco-Spanish allies. If he did not do so, Brazil would be borne off as a prize by the British, since what better opportunity could England have for possessing itself of the Azores, Madeira, all the colonies? He recalled the words that Lord Hankesbury had addressed to the French diplomat who was threatening him with the conquest of Lisbon and Oporto in case the English did not abandon Malta and be content with the Island of Ceylon: "If Napoleon invades Portugal, England will invade Portugal's overseas colonies. It will take the Azores and Brazil, two pawns which will be worth much more to it than continental Portugal will be to France." [2]

Caught between two fires, the tiny kingdom in either case would end by being crushed through the exigencies of geography. The thing to do was to choose the lesser of two evils, and accordingly he decided on Brazil. Later, when the storm had passed, he might return to Portugal with enhanced prestige owing to the great empire which he meant to found in that barbarous new land. And so the order was given, "Prepare to embark!" There was not a minute to be lost. The fury of the dread Corsican was ready to burst upon them. "Do not believe the regent of Portugal," the Little Corporal had said, "even when he promises to make war on England." In compliance with these directions, Junot had crossed the Bidassoa range by forced marches and was headed for Lisbon. With him were the veterans of Austerlitz, Kellermann's battalions, and Taviel's artillery, nearly twenty thousand men in all.

"Prepare to embark!" What a scurrying there was! Feverish preparations on every hand amid an indescribable hubbub. Prince John wished to take everything with him: the ministerial archives, the crown jewels, the royal silverplate, John V's carriages, the books from the library at Ajuda, the friars who were his personal attendants, the hangings from his country house, and whole trunks full of bric-a-brac.

It was pouring rain on that memorable morning of November 27, 1807. All Lisbon was a swarming ant heap as people went about with mud-spattered bundles under their arms. The nobility was engaged in dismantling its handsome residences and stuffing its precious belongings into trunks and hampers. There was Angeja in his house at Junqueira; there was Lavradio, who lived in the Campo de Santa Clara; there was Pombal on his estate, Janelas Verdes; there were Alegrete, Torres-Novas, Pombeiro, Caparica, Redondo, Belmonte. It took two days for the emigrant multitude to embark. In the throng that finally boarded the ships were to be seen ministers of state, nobles of the realm, magistrates and other public officials, friars, soldiers, chaplains of the royal guards, stable grooms, overseas chamberlains, liveried servants, milk nurses, humble wardrobe mistresses, and disheveled dandies, all of them laden down with bundles of clothing, enormous bales of victuals, and shapeless packages wrapped up in the *London Register* or the *Gazeta de Lisboa*.

Livid of countenance, with her hands to her white throat, Dona Maria stubbornly refused to embark; and they almost had to drag her aboard, for she could not but think of Marie Antoinette and kept screaming that they were bearing her off to the guillotine. She was accompanied by the tiny Pedro, who, his eyes fairly popping out, stood there taking it all in, inasmuch as protocol made it absolutely imperative for the heir to the crown to witness the spectacle.

Junot, meanwhile, was rushing on, coming ever closer and closer. Already he had passed Abrantes and was making for Lisbon at top speed. An incessant downpour that deluged the highways threatened to hold up his advance, but by the 28th he was in Santarem. The royal fleet, still waiting for a wind, had not as yet been able to leave the harbor. Not until the 29th did it finally succeed in slowly getting under way, thanks to a favoring monsoon, leaving behind the towers of São Julião. By nightfall the vessels had still not cleared the bar. Junot was at Cartaxo when he received word that the royal family had embarked. It was late at night, and he leaped out of bed without any clothes on, crying: *"Sacrement et tonerre!"* [3] He insisted upon setting out at once, in spite of the water which came up to the horses' bellies, and on the 30th he entered Lisbon with a thousand grenadiers that were half starved and dropping from exhaustion. In the distance the white sails of the ships could be seen. The battery of Bom Sucesso, which had been captured by the Napoleonic troops, then opened fire in a furious but futile effort to halt the fugitives.

What was really happening was this: Portugal was moving to Brazil. The entire administrative machinery of the monarchy was packed away in the holds of those ships now crossing the Atlantic, and with it went a contingent of more than fifteen thousand persons. What a trick it was that John VI had played on the emperor of the French! They had thought to trap him as they had his father-in-law, Charles IV, or his brother-in-law, Ferdinand VII. They had sought to humiliate him by transforming him into a plaything of the Corsican adventurer. He was not so foolish after all, this sleepy, good-natured prince who was in the habit of licking his tongue at sight of a young cock done to a golden brown over the fire. Later, at St. Helena, Napoleon was to do full justice to this cunning master stroke: "He was the only one who ever tricked me."

CHAPTER TWO

UNDER THE TROPICAL SUN

When the brig *Voador* put in at Rio de Janeiro bringing word of the imminent arrival of the royal family, the count of Arcos, who was the viceroy, was overcome with surprise and emotion. Portugal invaded by the French and the regent in flight for Brazil with his princess, his heirs, his ministers, his nobles, and all those public functionaries, thousands upon thousands of persons! Could it be possible? How were they to provide suitable lodgings for such distinguished guests, seeing that Rio was no more than a colonial village of a little over fifty thousand inhabitants, without conveniences and without sanitation? In any case there was no time to be lost, as the regent might arrive at any moment, and so the count immediately set to work. He called a meeting of the council, and the most urgent measures were forthwith adopted.

The first problem was that of dwelling places, and for this there was but one solution: all the good houses must be vacated and placed at the disposition of the emigrees and the owners must be crowded into other and inferior structures. Whole bands of public officials at once went forth to scrawl up over entryways the famous letters "P.R.," constituting a laconic notice of eviction. Those letters indicated that the houses in question had been reserved for the prince regent, but the native of Rio, with

[15]

his proverbial sense of humor, proceeded to interpret them liter-
ally: "Ponha-se na rua!" (Get out into the street!) Everywhere
numerous crews were engaged in cleaning the streets, mowing
the grass along the highways, and whitewashing walls, in an un-
heard of and feverish anxiety for cleanliness and embellishment.

The old Bobadela mansion, dressed up as a palace, would accommodate the royal family, and it was now painted and repaired
until it looked like a new edifice. It was, however, rather small,
in view of the large household that surrounded the prince—the
maids, alone, totaled twenty-eight. D. Marcos de Noronha, the
viceroy, however, was nothing if not resourceful and proceeded
to render habitable the pestilential site next door where the jail
stood, the inmates being transferred to the Aljube prisons and
the two buildings connected by a glass-enclosed passageway.

In connection with this transformation of the jail into an annex
to the royal palace, a curious incident is related. In the course of
his crossing to America, Prince John was already nearing the
shores of Brazil when from a distance a sail was sighted and everyone assured him that the craft came from Rio de Janeiro. There
was great excitement aboard, for this was the first vessel they had
encountered in all the days they had been at sea. The boat that
carried the regent went swiftly forward to meet the stranger, for
they were all anxious for news of the colony. When the two ships
were alongside each other, standing prow to prow, the trumpeter
upon the regent's direction called out, "Do they know in Rio de
Janeiro that the court is coming there?"

"Yes," came the answer, "the brig *Voador* has arrived after
a voyage of a few weeks to advise us of that fact. Everyone knows
it and they are getting the jail ready to receive the royal family."

This information was like the bursting of a bomb. Prince John
was stunned by it and did not know what to think. "The jail?
Good heavens! What is the meaning of this?"

The council was hastily summoned, but no one was able to understand such nonsense as that. Fortunately, the former viceroy of Brazil, D. Fernando Portugal, was among those present and he made everything clear. Inasmuch as the jail was a huge edifice adjoining the viceregal residence, Dom Marcos must have decided to make use of it by way of increasing the size of the house in which the royal family was to be installed.[1]

On the morning of March 7th the imposing royal fleet, with bellying sails and all its flags and pennants fluttering in the breeze, appeared opposite Sugar Loaf Mountain. Hundreds of small boats, galleys, and sloops, bearing the viceroy and other officials and important personages of the colony, promptly surrounded the Portuguese vessels as they cast anchor off Snake Island amid the booming of cannon and the enthusiastic cheers of the populace that packed the beaches, the quays, and the neighboring mountainsides. Leaning over the ship's rail, the fugitive court was fascinated by the opulence of the tropical landscape: the cluster of white houses clinging to the hillside slopes, the enormous granite palisades lashed by the sea, and the dense growth of forest on every hand, a veritable orgy of green tones and half-tones. The nobles of the realm, after so many weeks of privation, discomfort, and promiscuity, could at last breathe freely once again as they gazed on the city that was to be their host for more than thirteen long years.

Some of the ships, including the *Royal Prince,* which bore the regent and some sixteen hundred persons, had previously put in at Bahia, where the sovereign had first set foot on the soil of his vast American dominions. He was delighted with the fervent reception which the Bahians gave him. Never had his European subjects made him feel so loved and respected, and he could not but think of this as petition after petition was presented to him requesting that he bestow upon his city of São Salvador * the honor of residing there. He had come like a beggar expelled from his kingdom, with a vague remorse gnawing at his conscience for having abandoned his people to the French invader, but these townspeople made him forget all his troubles with their clamorous show of affection, their unreserved generosity, and the blind admiration they accorded him.

Among the addresses of welcome was one that especially impressed Prince John and had the effect of shaking him out of his inborn lethargy. It was delivered by José da Silva Lisboa, a liberal economist with enlightened ideas, of the school of Ricardo and Adam Smith. Speaking slowly and clearly, with cool reasoning and well knit logic, the illustrious Bahian went on to depict for the monarch the real situation of a country that was being asphyxiated by ancient laws and charters that hindered its growth and expansion and strangled its economy and foreign trade. The prince, if he would, might afford relief by opening its ports to friendly nations, thereby stimulating the rapid growth of Brazil, to the greater glory and enrichment of the Portuguese crown itself.

Impressed by the orator's weighty arguments, Prince John came near interrupting him—he would sign the decree that instant! The dyspeptic Braganza of old was no longer recognizable. In the past he had always hesitated, had had to consult his ministers and hear what his councilors had to say, but now, for the first time, he made a spontaneous decision of his own. Let them draw up the decree at once. This was done, and on that afternoon of the 18th of January, 1808, with a fateful show of courage, the regent put his name to one of the most important documents in Brazilian history. In a certain sense, this was the beginning of the country's independence.

* Bahia.

A charter of 1785 had prohibited manufactures in Brazil in order that the mother country might not lose an assured market, but Prince John annulled this with a stroke of his pen. Industry was now free. He went on to equalize the rights of nationals and foreigners and thus facilitated the arrival of the first European immigrants. The new land was now to emerge from the shades of colonial oppression. Having lost North America, and being unable to get much from the Orient, England must turn to Brazil for her supplies; and it was not long until British merchant vessels were laden down with Brazilian cotton, sugar, coffee, and hides. In the year 1807, Rio de Janeiro had been visited by ninety ships, the following year there were 420. The port of Bahia alone, in 1818, gave anchorage to some 2,000. Agriculture and commerce started to pick up, and the colony began to assert itself as a nation.

The disembarkment of the multitude of emigrees at Rio was witnessed by the Brazilians with the most intense curiosity. With what astonishment did they gaze at those women with the high waistlines and low-necked gowns and the men with their high-breasted trousers, their dress coats, and their periwigs. Nothing, however, surprised them so much as the clipped hair of the Portuguese women, a habit which they looked upon as being altogether reprehensible. It was only later that they learned that this was a sanitary measure rendered necessary by trying conditions aboard ship during the long crossing: it was the only means of doing away with certain small parasites. Many of the Rio women, none the less, in their eagerness to imitate what they supposed to be the Lisbon mode, hastened to cut off their own luxuriant tresses.

The obese Prince John, in his well worn, glossy swallowtail, attracted the attention of everyone, as did the skinny and angular

Dona Carlota, with her flat chest and sloping shoulders, and with that growth of down standing out darkly on her lean face. The princess was feeling morose and in a very bad humor as they left the ship, and the young princes, Dom Pedro and Dom Miguel, also appeared to be uneasy as they gazed in open-eyed wonderment at all the people bowing so reverently and wonderingly before them. In the cortege were: the royal princesses; the young Spanish prince, Don Pedro Carlos de Bourbon; the elegant Dona Maria Teresa; the princess of Brazil; the venerable widow of Prince Joseph; and any number of governesses and ladies in waiting. They all formed a long procession which now set out on foot for the Cathedral of the Rosary, where a solemn "Te Deum" was to be sung.

At the head walked Prince John beneath a sumptuous panoply, and a good portion of the public brought up the rear. The streets were strewn with flowers and leaves and adorned with arches in commemoration of the event, and the houses were covered from top to bottom with multicolored tapestries and streamers, while traditional bands of music were stationed at various points along the line of march.

It was not until three days later that the mad queen came ashore amid a general silence. There were no salvos of artillery this time, since these might frighten her, and it was a downcast sovereign who finally appeared, her hair flowing loosely, her pale face covered with her delicate hands. It was one of the intervals in those tragic fits of hallucination to which Her Majesty, Dona Maria I, queen of Portugal, Brazil, and the Algarves, was subject. Her journey from the quay to the Carmelite Convent where she was to be lodged occasioned great consternation on the part of the natives, who were dumfounded by the spectacle.

The prestige conferred by the presence of the monarch and the royal family, together with the elevation of the city to the rank of capital of all the realm, caused the Brazilians to forget in their rejoicing all the discomforts and mass evictions they had suffered in order to accommodate the arrogant nobles and impertinent functionaries, not to speak of the expense they had incurred and the new taxes with which the government was compelled to burden them. The regent, mild and benevolent and readily accessible to all, won the hearts of his subjects and came to be really esteemed by the populace. Dona Carlota, on the other hand, was generally hated by reason of her violent ways and the coarse and contemptuous invectives she employed in speaking of the country and its inhabitants.

A clever politician and ambitious for renown and undisputed authority, courageous when it came to action and cruel in exacting vengeance, she was the real leader of the Portuguese absolutists and continued to be until death took her off after thirty years of conspiring and intriguing against her husband, her brother, her son, and even her granddaughter, the little Princess Maria da Gloria. The thick black hair that covered her arms and dried-up face bespoke her masculine, headstrong character. Her massive reddish nose, coarse pimply skin, her big sparkling eyes and narrow mouth that could not conceal her ill cared for teeth —all these traits justified the witty remark of the duchess of Abrantes, who had spoken of her as "one of nature's marvels."

A hot-blooded person, she led a life filled with amorous adventures. The chroniclers of the period are scandalized as they inquire into the paternity of her offspring and speak of her gallery of kept favorites, whom she picked from among all classes of society, from the coachman Santos and the overseer of Ramalhão to the elegant and refined marquis de Marialva. In connection with these annals, the wife of a French ambassador at Lisbon observed: "The interesting thing about the royal family of Portugal is that one child never resembles a brother or sister." And now

Dona Carlota was in Brazil, "land of Negroes and of lice." She had come against her will and, homesick for Madrid, was, accordingly, filled with boredom and ill humor. The intense heat, the simplicity of the life that was led there, and the discomforts of the city made her quiver with indignation.

Rio de Janeiro in 1808 was, indeed, a dirty and uncomfortable city, obviously ill adapted to receiving so unlooked for an avalanche of princes and refined noblemen. In general the houses were a replica of the Portuguese style of the epoch: low-built, rambling, with usually but one floor, and with smooth white walls, rough-tiled roofs, narrow windows, and in the front, on a level with the ground, a wide wooden door. There were few façades that did not exhibit this same severe aspect, though their architectural lines were in better taste, being set off with balconies of the Florentine, Moorish, or Spanish variety. In the center there was usually a patio of Andalusian design, with doors or windows that afforded access to the rooms. Dutch tiling was the favorite decoration of churches, convents, and the vestibules of the better class homes, and was sometimes to be found in the more luxurious patios in place of the ordinary stone slabs.

In the narrow, ill paved streets, Dona Carlota was impressed by the Negroes who went by with large pails or baskets on their heads. They came from all the African races: Kaffirs, Quiloas, Malês, Benguellas, Monjolos, and had been picked up in Mozambique, in Guinea, in Angola, or along the coast of Mina, having been brought to Brazil to perform those heavy tasks which the Indian shunned and to which the white-skinned colonial never stooped. At the various fountains of the city, the Negroes with their pails would jostle one another for a chance to collect the scant and precious liquid. Their voices had an intense quality and their barbarous unintelligible idiom was accompanied by violent gestures. From time to time the scene would take on the appearance of a street brawl, interrupted by the hiss of the over-seer's lash. The blacks would then waddle off as the water from their pails dripped down over the coarse clouts which they wore tightly wrapped about the kinky wool of their heads.

Transportation was a dangerous and difficult affair. Coaches drawn by two or four horses, with liveried servants up behind and glass-paned windows, were few in number and a prerogative of the rich. Animal-borne litters with a trunk-shaped roof were more common, as were sedan chairs which had damask curtains and were carried by sturdy Negroes; and here was also the *serpentina,* a kind of Indian palanquin covered with cloth and adorned with rude carvings. Despite the scorching sun, Negro litter-bearers, when in the service of the nobility or the rich, must wear showy liveries consisting of heavy gilt-embroidered tunics, fine wigs, and white gloves; but in contrast to this display of elegance, their feet were always bare, for the white master never succeeded in imposing either sandals or shoes upon the African. Their bodies might be submissive, but the slaves insisted upon keeping their feet rustically free and unencumbered.

It was France that dictated the fashions for Portuguese and Brazilians alike. The men wore long swallow-tailed coats, silk waistcoats, tight-fitting trousers of every shade, neckcloths of white lace, shoes that were shaped like a water spout, with a high instep and enormous buckles, and finally, a three-cornered hat of beaver or of silk, which out of affectation was carried under the arm by persons of quality. The man in the street, or native, invariably wore a broad-brimmed Spanish hat, sandals without stockings and, even in the heat of summer, an ample greatcoat that covered his entire body; he also carried a sword, frequently unsheathed.

The women were quite as slavish as the men in imitating the Parisian *dernier cri.* They wore very tall wigs supported by an

iron framework which sometimes weighed more than fifteen
pounds, and from these grotesque coiffures they were accustomed
to suspend small household objects such as scissors, knives,
feathers, ribbons, and even vegetables.[2] Furnished on the inside
with a stout kid lining that fitted over their heads, these wigs
from lack of adequate support were almost always held in place
by means of fish glue or some other paste. As might readily have
been foreseen in such a climate, it was not long before the hot
sweat had melted the glue, causing it to run down over the face
of the fashionable ladies, while the unpleasant odor was to be
perceived a long way off.

The women almost never went out except to attend Mass,
very rarely for visits or balls, and when they did so they were
enveloped in flowing mantillas of serge or lacework. As for hoop
skirts with whalebone stays, they had been deflated since the
French Revolution. In the time of Prince John and Doña Carlota,
the women were already beginning to wear the "imperial girdle,"
and their gowns were becoming more and more form-fitting.
They were systematically kept illiterate, and their crass ignorance
was celebrated in certain popular refrains:

> The lass who knows too much
> Doth make a sorry show;
> The mother of a family
> Should little or nothing know.

This was, assuredly, not the ideal environment for the daughter of Charles IV of Spain, and she was unable to conceal or soften
her ill humored impressions of the country. Her one pleasure consisted of a daily outing through the better kept suburban streets,
either alone or with her daughters. Exaggeratedly jealous of her
royal prerogatives, she was accompanied by a pair of truculent
grooms on horseback whose function it was to demand at the

point of the sword that homage that she felt was rightly hers.

The representatives of foreign powers, feeling that their diplomatic prerogatives were being encroached upon, sought to flee such a humiliation; but this was in no wise pleasing to the haughty princess. Consuls, legation secretaries, and even ambassadors found themselves rudely compelled to dismount from their coaches or their steeds and pay their compliments to the sovereign. The Russian ambassador, Baron Tuyll, a polished gentleman averse to unpleasant incidents, deemed it the part of prudence to give up the house in which he was living in the Laranjeiras quarter, since this was one of the princess's favorite haunts; he preferred to lose the 40,000 francs which he had expended in improving the property. Nor did the mighty and imposing Lord Strangford, representing His Britannic Majesty, escape the exigencies of this rigid ceremonial. In 1814, at the edge of a road, he was punished for his reluctance by one of the princess' men, who gave him a severe pommeling and hauled him down off his horse. Brushing off the dust that stained his impeccable frock coat, the apoplectic diplomat could only stand there fuming and hurling threats at the attendant as the latter rode off on the gallop. Never had an English lord suffered such an affront!

His fellow countryman, Commodore Bowles, head of a naval detachment that was passing through Rio, also had the misfortune to fall in with Dona Carlota's coach. Aware of preceding incidents, he quickly sought to flee the highway and made for a sidepath but did not succeed in reaching it. Divining his intention, the outriders stopped him in his tracks and beat him with the flat of their swords as a punishment for the insult he had offered the lady. More ingenious and daring than others, the United States minister, Sumter, was the only one who succeeded in avoiding the disagreeable experience. Seeing that diplomatic

protests had failed to achieve the desired result, he armed himself with a good brace of pistols, and when the attendants as-
saulted him, he pointed the weapons at their bosoms, coolly
threatening to shoot at the first move they made against him.
Infuriated by his audacity, Dona Carlota called out to the men to
give him a thrashing; but those eloquent pistols, wielded with
such firmness, had a paralyzing effect upon the aggressors, who
finally retired despite the vehement insults which their mistress
heaped upon them.

Only then did Prince John make up his mind expressly to
exempt foreigners from paying to the royal family any form of
tribute other than that which was customary in their respective
countries. He thus put an end to the abuse, but many of the results were irremediable, such as the loss of those 40,000 francs
on the part of that prudent and refined gentleman, the baron of
Tuyll.

Ever since 1806, the year in which Prince John unmasked the
plans of Dona Carlota to snatch his crown from him by means
of a palace coup, the royal pair had lived in a state of practical
separation. At Rio, the princess and her daughters occupied the
urban palace and, later, a house situated in Botafogo, a picturesque
seaside suburb, while the regent, with his two sons and his
nephew, went to reside at the pleasant country palace of São
Cristovão, which had been presented to the monarch by a rich
merchant, Elias Lopes, and which stood in the midst of a grove
of beautiful leafy trees. Court life was marked by an extreme
simplicity. As made over by the count of Arcos, the Rio palace
was a spacious mansion but one that left much to be desired; the
worm-eaten woodwork creaked here and there and the walls had
been too hastily plastered. As for São Cristovão, it was large
enough and had a huge veranda supported by twenty columns,
but it did not differ from other rural homes in Brazil; it was not

until eight years afterward that it was given a more luxurious appearance.

The sovereign rose at six o'clock in the morning and, in company with his inseparable companion Lobato, went to say his prayers in the royal chapel. Then, as he breakfasted on his favorite dish of tender young cocks, he received those nobles with whom he was on terms of greater intimacy and a few functionaries. Dinner was from two to three and was a solemn occasion. The prince ate with his sons and nephew, surrounded by chamberlains, overseers, physicians, and officials of the household. As dessert was brought in, there was the ceremony of the washing of hands, with Dom Pedro holding the silver basin, Dom Miguel the water pitcher, and the little Dom Sebastião the towel. After that the sovereign napped for an hour or more. About five in the afternoon he went out for a ride in his carriage and did not return until the stroke of the Ave Maria, when he repaired to his study at São Cristovão to look over papers and attend to affairs of state. He went to sleep around eleven.[3]

Each day he paid a visit to the mad queen. She received him sometimes with indifference and at other times with a show of affection as she contrived to articulate a few lucid sentences; but if anyone else happened to approach her, she would hide her face with her hands and cry out that while she might be on the road to hell she preferred to avoid the sight of the devil.

Prince John especially enjoyed spending some time on his Santa Cruz plantation, an estate near Rio that had formerly belonged to the Jesuits; or it might be Governor's Island, in the middle of Guanabara Bay, at a convent of Benedictine monks that had been made over for his comfort at a cost of 100,000 cruzados.* He was also fond of going to the islands of Paquetá and Bom Jesus, in his galley with the silken awning; on such

* Approximately $450,000 at the present rate.

occasions he took pleasure in watching the rowers in their silver helmets and scarlet velvet cloaks as he sat there breathing deeply with his thick hair floating on the breeze.

Here in the sun the apathetic Braganza felt happy, freed to an extent of those morbid family troubles that had tormented him in his gloomy palace at Lisbon. Jovial and benevolent, he proceeded to democratize court ceremonies, including that of kissing the royal hand. Seated in his study and surrounded by red-clad officers of his guard with their silver halberds, he gave audience to all without distinction as to social class: farmers, priests, backlanders, slave dealers, men of the people. Back in Portugal, in the palace of Ajuda, he had been a false divinity, inaccessible and artificial. Here he was at once father, judge, counselor, in direct contact with his people who understood and respected him.

In the past the arts and crafts had been looked upon as plebeian pursuits, and the descendants of anyone who had engaged in such an occupation were forbidden to hold public office down to the third generation; but now these callings were raised to the same dignity that the other professions enjoyed. Breaking with century-old tradition, Prince John now began granting patents of nobility to progressive individuals among the merchant classes and conferred upon them decorations and other honors. America was exalting human labor and working toward the equality of men.

CHAPTER THREE

THE EDUCATION OF A PRINCE

The education of Portuguese princes was almost wholly neglected, and it had been thought that all John needed, as a second son, was a smattering of Latin and theology instilled into him by the friars in whose company he had spent his melancholy childhood and colorless adolescence. Seeing that he was not destined for the throne, why trouble to give him broader notions of history, geography, or political science? Upon the death of the heir, Prince Joseph, to whom all had looked with such great expectations, the scepter had fallen into John's inexperienced hands, and he had wielded it gropingly and hesitatingly, tormented always by doubts and guided solely by that "proverbial craftiness of the peasant" which the Portuguese writer Herculano discovered in him.

He accordingly did not seek for his sons any more extensive training than he himself had received. Both Dom Pedro, heir to the crown, and Dom Miguel were brought up haphazardly, without giving any concern to their complacent father and licentious mother. Being of an exuberant temperament, both fled their tutors in order to mingle with stable boys and spent their days with the street urchins of the vicinity, whose habits and jargon they readily picked up. Of a somewhat less expansive nature than Dom Pedro, Dom Miguel was closer to his mother, who adored and protected him, and he at times kept his distance from a brother whose wild exploits tired him and whose daring he secretly envied.

As a result of this intimacy with street urchins, Dom Pedro grew up with no respect for the symbols and conventions of his age. At gala ceremonies, when the young nobles, faithful to the laws of etiquette, would bend to kiss the back of his hand, he would suddenly give them a slap on the chin, being barely able to restrain his laughter at sight of the stupefied look on their faces. He felt himself to be a son of the people rather than of royalty, and all his life long he was to be on cordial and familiar terms with individuals of every walk in life. His best friend, and confidential secretary, was a groom of the wardrobe commonly known as "Chalaça," or the Jester, who later became the Councilor Francisco Gomes da Silva. Another of his intimates, João Carlota, came out of the pantry at São Cristovão; and upon Dom Pedro's orders a former scavenger, Plácido de Abreu, became no less a personage than treasurer of the imperial household. It was company of this kind that molded his youthful tastes.

The prince's great-grandfather had liked to measure his strength in bodily contests with his servants; and similarly, after he had become emperor, Dom Pedro once grappled with a corpulent state functionary who, while in his cups, had maintained that his sovereign could not throw him. On another occasion, when "Chalaça" was involved in a tavern brawl, the royal heir came running up to rescue his companion with blows of his fists. Exhibiting the same fury that he did in chastizing with his riding whip the remissness of a public functionary, he would hasten to free a slave who was being mistreated by his master. Hearing a fire alarm near by, he would go on the run in the company of the first citizen he encountered to help put out the flames. On the other hand, if he felt that some diplomat, the representa-

tive of a great power, deserved a haughty and arrogant reply, no
one could be more overbearing and sharp-tongued than he.

Strong of body and endowed with an impetuous disposition,
Dom Pedro none the less early manifested a keen intelligence,
and this, by awakening in him a desire for knowledge, was to
save him from being wholly uncultivated. Of the tutors that
they gave him, one only, João Rademaker, succeeded in arousing
the young prince's interest by his cleverness in explaining the
subject in hand through illuminating example and suggestive
comparisons. A scholar and a linguist, the former Portuguese
minister to Denmark and at Buenos Aires, by reason of his ex-
ceptional competence might have carried the moral and scientific
training of his ward much further had not death—he was poi-
soned by a Negro slave girl—come to interrupt suddenly a task
that had been so auspiciously begun.

Without any particular form of restraint such as would compel
them to study (it was said that Prince John had ordered the tutors
not to bother the lads), the youths might give free rein to their
natural inclinations, which were toward a life in the open air,
physical exercises, horseback riding, and the like. Above all, they
were thus able to find outlet for those plebeian instincts that they
had inherited from Alfonso VI, through their daily familiarity
with lackeys or other sturdy specimens of the lower classes. On
the Santa Cruz plantation Pedro and Miguel fought real battles
at the head of bands of young slaves armed with clubs and wooden
muskets; and already in these combats, which he always won,
the former gave evidence of that military genius that he later displayed on the hard-fought battlefields of Portugal, where the
same princes commanded opposing armies in a bloody, fratricidal
struggle without truce or quarter.

Debret, the French artist who lived in Rio de Janeiro, in his

Voyage pittoresque, has described for us a victorious charge of Negro lads under the prince's command; they had fallen upon a station of the royal guard near São Cristovão, and there was nothing for the soldiers to do but flee the valiant assault.

Dom Pedro was also a daring horseman, accustomed from earliest infancy to handling the royal palfreys, and there was soon not a professional equestrian to be found anywhere who was better versed than he in the art of bit and saddle. At São João del Rey, the stablemen stood open-mouthed as they watched him, barefoot and clad in calico trousers, break in with all the skill of an expert the animals they had given him to ride.[1] He was proud of his ability in everything that had to do with horses, and loved to exhibit it. Once while riding through the suburbs of Rio he came upon a man who, drawn up alongside the road, was endeavoring unsuccessfully to shoe his mount. Leaping to the ground, the prince drove in the nails for him like one who had practiced the trade for years. Again, he reined in at a blacksmith's door and ordered the fellow to put on a shoe. The smith had barely begun when Dom Pedro stopped him saying: "Get out of the way, you swine, you don't know your business!" Saying this, he took the tools and in the blink of an eye performed the job in masterly fashion.[2]

Handsome, virile, self-confident in his bearing, with his mother's sensuality showing in his blunt manner toward women, the young prince was soon to be the talk of the town by reason of his amorous feats of prowess. A tropical Don Juan, something of a throwback to his lusty grandfather, John V, he would plunge forth into the night, muffled up like a conspirator, in search of gallant adventures. Riding along on horseback, he would sometimes go so far as to draw back the curtains of passing litters or coaches, in search of beautiful ladies.

A certain actress by the name of Ludovina, for whom he had conceived a passion, decided to play a trick upon him. When, fairly bursting with eagerness, he put in an appearance at their nocturnal rendezvous, she received him smilingly and led him into the house, where her companions of the theater were all standing around holding lighted tapers, awaiting the honor of His Royal Highness's visit. Perceiving that he had been made the victim of a jest, he was not angry but carried the thing off with great good humor.

The diplomatic representatives stationed in Rio, in the dispatches sent to their governments, frequently speak of Dom Pedro's amours in a way that violates the matter-of-fact austerity of chancellery archives. Certain communications of the French minister have the unmistakable flavor of vaudeville. Others speak of the young prince's fickleness: "The objects of his gallantry, a new one each week, are chosen from among Brazilian, Italian, French, and even Spanish-American ladies, but none seems able to hold his affections!" His escapades were already being talked of in the salons of Europe, and one correspondent wrote back that he was "very frisky with the ladies." Having received from the chief of police a respectful account of how his son was carrying on, Prince John was embarrassed and sought to avoid scandal by remunerating the victims or marrying them off to loyal officers of his guard; but the fact none the less became known, and the entire city amused itself by discussing in every tone of voice the gay nights Dom Pedro spent.

Endowed with an artistic temperament, the prince, in spite of his irregular upbringing, was to exhibit a surprising bent toward music, drawing, sculpture, the manual crafts, and even poetry. Music was for him a kind of hereditary necessity. Both his father and grandfather had conducted orchestras, being as passionately fond of the Gregorian chant as was his great-great-grandfather, who had founded a school of church music at São José de Ribamar, thus perpetuating a trait that derived from "Peter I, who played the cornet, to John IV, who played all instruments." [3] Under the direction of José Maurício and Marcos Portugal, who had taught him the rudiments of the art, Dom Pedro was able to play with some degree of skill not only the flute and violin, but the bassoon and trombone as well.

He was not unfamiliar with the theories of composition, harmony, and counterpoint, which had been taught him by Sigismund von Neukomm, favorite disciple of Haydn, who was Beethoven's teacher. Various compositions that were sung in his father's chapel and later in the imperial chapel of Brazil were of his authorship, and he very frequently acted as conductor. Jacques Arago, French novelist and playwright, who chanced to enter the royal chapel in Rio, was greatly impressed by the character of the music he heard there, rendered under the prince's baton and composed by him. [4]

Years later in Paris, after he had abdicated the throne of Brazil, he was to become the intimate friend of Rossini, who very often sought him out to converse on musical subjects and submit his own works to His Majesty's judgment. Rossini, in fact, was so taken with one of Dom Pedro's symphonies that he had it performed by the orchestra of the Théâtre Italien, an event that took place on October 30, 1831, and met with the greatest success.

The versatility of this prince who had had so little schooling was really quite out of the ordinary. Although lacking in method and direction, he loved to dally with the arts and sciences, being moved by an instinctive and eager curiosity. The impressive thing about him is the combination of diverse tendencies, of brutality and subtlety, of manual and intellectual interests, of theory and practice, of sublimity and depravity. In his letters, characterized by a barbarous syntax and uncertain spelling, one frequently comes upon Latin quotations which he had remembered from the haphazard instruction given him by Friar Antônio de Arrabida. He liked to practice his beginner's French upon the diplomats and cite the latest authors that had come to hand. He read with avidity the works of Benjamin Constant and was enthusiastic over General Foy's addresses. The French consul Maler found him leafing through a volume of Edmund Burke which he thought of translating and publishing in *The Mirror* of Rio. But he was conscious of the deficiencies in his education and would jestingly remark that he and his brother Miguel were "the last ignoramuses of the family."

In crafts such as cabinetmaking and wood turning, he was outstanding. The Reverend Robert Walsh mentions the carpenter's shop where the prince labored and expresses deep surprise at having witnessed a display of his handiwork. Innumerable objects have come down to attest his dexterity: a miniature ship complete in every detail; a perfectly finished billiard table; a bust of himself which he had carved as a figurehead for the frigate *Dom Pedro I;* a wooden crown for the Empress Leopoldina's bier and the carving for her rosewood mausoleum which may be viewed to this day in St. Anthony's Convent at Rio de Janeiro. Writing to the governor of Bahia on affairs of state, he is suddenly mindful of the needs of his workshop and includes in his letter a request for sixteen different varieties of wood.

Equipped solely with his intelligence, his intuition, and his courage, to make up for the culture that he lacked, this prince was destined to play a great historic role. He was to found an empire at the age of twenty-four and oversee the drawing up of two constitutions; confronting the Holy Alliance, he was to free Portugal of absolutism, securing for his sons the thrones of their two fatherlands; and finally—the only instance of its kind in history—he was to renounce for himself four crowns: that of Brazil, which he won; that of Portugal, which he inherited; and those of Spain and Greece, which were offered him. As if foreseeing that the time allotted him was short, Dom Pedro lived his thirty-six years at a dizzy pace. His life was full of unforeseen and impulsive acts, sudden turns of fortune and explosive incidents and commotions, but it was a life the echoes of which were to live on like a bold and heroic clarion call long after it was finished.

CHAPTER FOUR

AUSTRIAN ARCHDUCHESS

Dom Pedro's marriage was a trump card of which John VI meant to make clever use in getting the monarchy out of difficulties. Already, in 1807, he had attempted to appease Napoleon by offering the hand of the young prince, then only nine years old, to Murat's daughter, the emperor's niece. When this plan went astray, he decided to hold his trump for a better occasion.

As matters in the River Plate region became aggravated to the point where there existed a state of semibelligerency between the two Iberian powers, John felt that the moment had come to play the card another time. He now planned to marry off his heir to a Russian princess, a sister, it might be, of the powerful Alexander, czar of all the Russias. With such an alliance, he felt, he would be able to counter the pretensions of Spain and would be in a position to lay down the law in the Peninsula and throughout America. The diplomatic machinery was accordingly set in motion, and negotiations with the Muscovite sovereign were begun; but owing to an adverse set of circumstances, the match was not consummated. Meanwhile, the duke of Calabria, heir to the crown of the Two Sicilies, and the queen regent of Etruria were engaged in a lively dispute as to which should procure for his or her daughter the honor of having Dom Pedro for a husband.

John, however, paid little attention to them; the plan that he had in mind loomed much larger in his sight.

Wellington had swept Napoleon's grenadiers out of Portugal, and England as the price of its services had imposed upon the monarch of that country an almost absolute submission. An alliance with the house of Austria, counterbalancing the British influence, would restore Portugal to its former freedom of movement, so often shackled by its Britannic allies, who were invaluable in time of war but inconvenient in time of peace. The Austrian emperor, who had bestowed upon Napoleon his firstborn, Marie Louise, still had three daughters to dispose of: Clementine, Caroline, and Leopoldina. Why not pick one of those that were left? Had not the Emperor Leopold sent his daughter, Maria Ana, to Lisbon to wed John V, in 1708? John VI's plans went further than this. He was thinking, also, of marrying his daughter, Isabel-Maria, to the Austrian crown prince.

The chargé d'affaires in Vienna, Navarro de Andrade, received instructions to make the proper overtures. With shrewdness and tact the future baron of Vila-Seca approached Metternich and the state councilor Hudelist on the subject, sent up suitable trial balloons, and then formally laid the two proposals before them. The second one had to be abandoned because of the prince's physical condition, for although he was twenty-three years old, "he gave not the faintest sign of any virile disposition or inclinations suitable to such an age." On the other hand, Navarro did succeed in interesting Metternich very much in the plan for marrying Dom Pedro to one of the archduchesses. The difficulties in the way were considerable. The two oldest ones, Clementine and Leopoldina, had already been promised respectively to the Sicilian prince and to the king of Saxony's nephew. As for the youngest, Caroline, despite her fifteen years she was still physically so frail as to be a long way from puberty. However, the principal objective had been fully accomplished: Metternich's aid had been enlisted, and for him there were no insoluble problems. Indeed, he was not long in finding a way out. He would bestow Leopoldina upon the Brazilian prince and the king of Saxony's nephew would have to wait until the other princess was in a condition to marry.

These preliminaries having been settled, John resolved to send Marialva, then ambassador at Paris, to Vienna for the purpose of arranging the match and making a formal and solemn request. As he saw it, Austria was powerful and influential, the center of the Holy Alliance of European monarchs; but Portugal also had something to offer. The crown of the Braganzas represented the richest empire on the face of the earth. He would dazzle Vienna with the gold and diamonds of Brazil borne by an embassy whose luxurious display would astonish the courts of the older continent.

The official entry of Marialva into the Austrian capital, with "the retinue of a sultan and the pomp of the Holy Father," did indeed constitute a spectacle worthy of the *Arabian Nights*. All the inhabitants of the city hung out of windows or jostled one another on the sidewalks to watch the majestic procession as it passed. The emperor and empress themselves and other members of the imperial family went to Count von Althan's house near the Carinthia gate in order not to miss a single detail of the imposing sight.

The way was cleared by members of the royal guard on horseback. After them came the carriages of the ministers, councilors of state, and palace chamberlains, including eight princes and nine counts, each of the vehicles being drawn by six horses and attended by footmen clad in costly liveries. Then came the imperial coach with Navarro, Marialva's master of ceremonies, and the gentleman companion to Count von Wilschek.[1] Finally, the ambassador's coach appeared, preceded and accompanied by a brilliant array of servants, including pages, equerries, court messengers, footmen, keepers of the wardrobe, and officials of the royal household, "all of them in resplendent uniforms and mounted upon jennets caparisoned in cloth of gold and scarlet, embroidered with the coat of arms of the Menezes Coutinhos." Bringing up the rear were the ambassadors of Spain, England, and France, and then two more of Marialva's carriages handsomely adorned with showy tinsel.

And so the proud marquis well might inform his king: "There had never before been seen in Vienna so sumptuous an embassy."

On the following day the formal request for the Princess Leopoldina's hand was made in accordance with the complicated rules of court ceremonial. "Having been brought from his residence to the palace, the marquis was conducted past the long row of imperial guards lining the stairway to the salons above, where another guard consisting of German and Hungarian noblemen was stationed. All the ministers and councilors of state, the high officials of the crown, the princes, and a large part of the nobility then filed in to the Hall of Knights, whence the lord steward accompanied the ambassador to the throne room." [2]

Beneath a rich canopy Francis I was waiting, clad in a field marshal's uniform. After the customary salutations had been exchanged, the marquis delivered an appropriate address and was delighted to hear the emperor grant his consent. In accordance with etiquette, the princess was called in to give her confirmation, both orally and in writing. She appeared at once, radiantly happy, for she had been passionately in love with Dom Pedro ever since she gazed on his portrait which Marialva had shown her. She had remarked at the time, with timid modesty, that "the features in that portrait were very much in conformity with the idea she had conceived of the moral virtues possessed by the august original." Marialva, with his gentlemanly smile, informed her that she was quite right in thinking this; and then he mentally recalled those pleasant pastimes of the restless heir to the throne, who at that very moment was being valiantly initiated into love's mysteries with the aid of all the French modistes in Rio de Janeiro.

Shortly before, Leopoldina had made certain discreet inquiries of the Portuguese chargé d'affaires in Vienna, and that well mannered courtier, knowing that the natural sciences were a monomania with the princess, did not hesitate to assure her that those were, precisely, the studies in which Dom Pedro was most interested. She had been barely able to refrain from an exclamation of delight. She must polish up her knowledge in order not to cut a sorry figure in the presence of her bridegroom, and she must take him a valuable collection of European minerals and a host of plants to be acclimated in Brazil.

Better than any other, Marialva knew how to make use of the authorization that had been sent him from Rio to draw upon the royal treasury for whatever sums were needed. They had also sent "various jewels and rich medals of honor for him to distribute, valued at £5,800, together with 167 diamonds to be set in those medals that were to be struck off in Europe, and seventeen bars of gold destined for certain persons who would be much more pleased to receive such a gift as this than other presents that were purely ornamental." Besides the sumptuous presents given to Metternich, his lieutenants, and the priest who celebrated the betrothal ceremony, Marialva further bestowed, in the form of money or of jewels, presents by the handful on the officials of the chancellery, chamberlains, ladies in waiting, physicians, chaplains, nobles of the guard, and pages and functionaries of every rank. There were watches with gold chains, rings, necklaces, medals, earrings, golden caskets, all of which the marquis distributed with an enthusiastic prodigality.

The present from the bridegroom was breathtaking. It was a portrait of Dom Pedro upon a beautiful medallion "framed in diamonds, with a crown above it, and suspended by a chain that was likewise of diamonds." The princess's waiting woman and major-domo were quite dazzled by the sight, remarking that they would never have believed that such wealth existed; and Metternich himself observed to Marialva that "only in fabulous tales of the Orient would one meet with a suitable description of such an object." [3]

In this manner, with presents and sumptuous banquets, the marquis succeeded in spending more than a million florins,* a notable amount for that age, not to mention 275,000 cruzados † which he had dispensed out of his personal fortune.

On May 13, 1817, John VI's birthday, the marriage was performed by proxy, the bridegroom being represented by the Archduke Charles. Marialva, who had already astounded Vienna with a ball given at his residence in commemoration of John's elevation to the throne, now resolved to celebrate the wedding with even greater pomp and splendor. Engineers and architects were called in and, under the direction of Charles Moreau, were ordered to erect upon the imperial estate at Augarten a palace capable of accommodating more than two thousand persons.

On July 1 the magnificent affair took place. The first guests began arriving at eight in the evening and were received by Marialva and by the wife of the Spanish ambassador, the duchess of San Carlos. Little by little the huge park was flooded with

* Approximately $2,500,000 at the present rate.
† Approximately $1,230,000 at the present rate.

light from a host of lanterns strung in the trees. To the gentle strains of orchestras stationed among the "flowering hedges and lordly foliage," the nobles and diplomats filed past, their embroidered dress coats agleam with medals; and there were also comely bands of Viennese ladies, with their white skins and alluring gait.

At nine o'clock the royal family put in an appearance, and immediately afterward, in the grand ballroom, the first notes of an animated polka were heard. Marialva invited Her Serene Highness, the princess, to dance with him, and together they proceeded to execute a number of elegant movements. The evening had begun. After the dances, supper. Amid the finest crystal and the richest porcelain, the guests were served from silver platters. At the table of honor, where the royal family supped, everything was of solid gold—knives, forks, and plates. Triumphantly Marialva observed the astonishment of his guests. It was truly a scene out of the *Thousand and One Nights*. Had not his sovereign ordered him to spend whatever was necessary? There was gold enough in Brazil to pay for it all.

Leopoldina was enchanted with the horizons that were opening before her, and sought to convince her friends: "Don't worry about the long voyage; for me there could be no greater pleasure in this world than that of going to America." To her aunt, the grand duchess of Tuscany, she remarked: "The voyage has no terrors for me. Indeed, I think it is a matter of fate, seeing that America has always had a singular attraction for me, and even as a child I used to say that I wanted to visit it some time." The emperor himself, many years later, was to observe to the marquis of Rezende: "It would appear that a special destiny summoned my daughter to America."

From Vienna, Leopoldina journeyed to Florence, where, domi-

ciled in the famous Pitti Palace, she awaited the arrival at Livorno
of the Portuguese ships that were to bear her to the New World.
On August 13th she embarked upon the *John VI,* where she was
received by the marquis of Castelo-Melhor, the Portuguese sovereign's special commissary. The princess was accompanied by a
varied and brilliant retinue, consisting of stewards, chamberlains,
six Hungarian noblemen, six Austrian guardsmen, a grand
almoner, a chaplain, a librarian, a botanist, a mineralogist, a
zoologist, an entomologist, and various artists, including the
painter Thomas Ender.

Matrimony in the life of the eighteen-year-old Dom Pedro
came as an unlooked for restraint on his free, hairbrained, dis-
orderly existence spent in the more turbulent quarters of the city.
His surprise upon receiving the news was followed by curiosity.
An Austrian archduchess for his wife, sister to the empress of
the French, sister-in-law to Napoleon! As he turned Leopoldina's
portrait over and over in his hand, his imagination was busy——

At five in the afternoon of November 5, 1816, the long-
expected fleet arrived at the entrance of the harbor. As the *John VI,*
the *Augusta,* and the *St. Sebastian* entered the bay with all sails
set, the fortresses and the new arrivals exchanged the customary
salute, their cannon thundering rhythmically in a mock naval
combat. From the Castelo hill a royal salute from the artillery
was followed by the bursting of rockets that filled the air with
thunder and drowned out the merry pealing of the bells. The
galley that conveyed the royal family, accompanied by a large
number of sloops laden with leading members of the nobility,
then rowed out to the *John VI* to welcome the princess. It was a
royal reception in every sense of the word.

Leaning heavily on the arm of the marquis of Castelo-Melhor,
Leopoldina, who was deeply moved by it all, descended to the
galley. As she was being affectionately embraced by their Maj-

esties, Dom Pedro, staring at her with wide-open eyes, was conscious of the greatest disappointment he had ever known in his life. He had expected a golden-haired blonde, sweet and pretty, and here they had sent him an erudite young lady carrying a collection of lepidoptera under her arm and eager for a discussion of mineralogical classifications.

A dozen years later, when a second wife was being sought for Pedro, the Austrian emperor was to say: "What my son-in-law needs is a bride who is beautiful and witty." Leopoldina, unfortunately, was neither one nor the other. Versed in the natural sciences, she was completely ignorant of the feminine art of pleasing. It had never occurred to her that cosmetics might have their uses, nor did she know anything of those innumerable resources that enable a woman to enhance her charms. Of medium stature and inclined to stoutness, she had blue eyes, a tiny nose, and a Hapsburg mouth with small protruding lips. With her wholesome red cheeks and heavy unattractive gait, she more nearly resembled a plump and rosy country maiden than anything else. Marialva himself, when he has to broach the delicate subject of the princess's physical endowments, displays a sobriety that leaves not the slightest doubt as to his real opinion. He limits himself to the statement that "in her presence sovereignty shines forth alongside the rarest virtue."

Dom Pedro right nobly concealed as best he could his real impression, but his princess on the contrary was unable to hide her satisfaction with the husband that had been given her. He was tall, elegant, of martial appearance, even handsomer than the portrait Marialva had shown her, and his sturdy bosom gleamed with showy stars and other military decorations. His general's uniform with a high embroidered collar that was grazed by his reddish whiskers suited him admirably well.

The city was gaily decked out to receive Her Most Serene Imperial

Highness. The artists Debret and Montigny had seen to the imposing decorations, which had completely transformed the aspect of the principal streets. Arches of triumph had been erected consisting of enormous columns with gilded capitals supporting inscriptions that alluded to the happy union of the two royal families. The windows of the houses were trimmed with varicolored silks and buntings and, in the words of an old chronicler, were occupied by "beautiful and richly adorned ladies, nearly all of whom held garlands of lovely, fragrant flowers which they were ready to strew upon the coach that bore Their Majesties and Royal Highnesses." For three whole days Rio preserved this festive aspect, its streets remaining covered with sand and sweet-smelling foliage, and from the doors and windows silken pennants and tapestries still fluttered. After dark the entire town was brilliantly illuminated for those three dreamlike nights. And then, everything was as it had been before, as the city resumed its customary appearance of a tranquil and not too clean overgrown country town.

Between bucolic distractions and domestic raptures, Leopoldina's first years in Brazil were pleasant ones. She would spend whole afternoons in the depths of the neighboring forest, classifying minerals, identifying rare plants, or merrily pursuing gaudy butterflies. Within the house, the mere presence of her husband filled her days with joy and happiness. A passion for music was one of the bonds that brought them together. Seated at the piano, she would accompany the prince, who was always ready to take up the flute or violin, or even to play the trombone or bassoon, with an equal virtuosity. In the absence of her "beloved consort," she would divulge her happiness to the world, to her father, her aunts, and other relatives in Vienna: "I do not have the words to tell you how happy I feel. . . . How pleasant it is to share with the person one loves so dearly the tranquil pleasures of the countryside which I am enjoying here."

Very soon her dreams are filled with the delights of maternity. The first time she feels a touch of nausea, she writes to her family: "It is a good sign! It appears that my ardent desires are to be realized!" On this occasion it was no more than a matter of over-eating on the part of one ill accustomed to the seasonings of the country, but the day was not long in coming when she was able to announce with pride: "The blessed event is to occur at the end of March." To her aunt Louisa Amelia she had confided, some months before: "I can already appreciate, without having experienced it, the pleasure of being a mother."

She was certain that the child would be a boy, as she informed everyone; but on April 4th, 1819, in place of a male heir the princess Maria da Gloria, future queen of Portugal, was born. Beside herself with joy, Leopoldina was not concerned with the fact that her expectations had not been realized. The important thing was to become a mother, God be praised! A new and in-evitable theme now occurs in her letters: "I have spent the entire day with my little daughter on my lap, watching her slightest movements and desires; she is so strong that she can already sit up and lift her head without help." The royal mother grows more and more exultant: "My little daughter is the loveliest and most intelligent child that I know; she is already beginning to prattle and to stand, for she has an extraordinary strength in her legs." Further on she adds: "When we are at home, all we do is carry her about in our arms. She has hair like mine, but that is all; in every other way she is the image of my husband, which renders her doubly dear to me."

Nothing was more important than maternity for Leopoldina. Again she writes to her father: "It appears that I am once more expecting." In an uninterrupted series of communications, she goes on to keep him informed of the progress of her pregnancy, step by step: "I am in my third month. . . . I am in my fourth month. . . . I am in my fifth month. . . . I expect to be delivered in February."

She adored animals. Wild or domestic, she treated them with equal interest and affection. This is constantly evident in her correspondence. In April, 1822, in a letter describing for her father the "terrible situation," politically speaking, in Brazil, a letter filled with worries and anxieties, she inserts a parenthesis: "Pohl has brought me a cub, a cross between a lion and a panther, a rare bird from China, a she-mule that has offspring, an ox with a Tartary hump, as well as many other animals and a couple of Botocudo Indians who live near here and I should not care to part with any of them."

On May 16, 1825, she is closing a letter to the "excellent Schaeffer," her European agent, when she happens to recall the needs of her zoological garden; and so she adds a postscript: "Send me two badger hounds and a dog that knows how to dive." Nor was Schaeffer the only one who received such requests. She frequently asked her imperial father for new specimens for her collection: "To change the subject, I would request of you six Transylvanian horses for breeding purposes." When she wished to make someone a nice present, she would forward him an assortment of animals. On December 12, 1822, desirous of wheedling her father, she gives him the gratifying news: "I have a few monkeys and other beasts to send you upon the first occasion that offers."

CHAPTER FIVE

WHO WILL GO: FATHER OR SON?

The long sojourn of the court in Brazil was profoundly displeasing to the Portuguese. The Corsican tyrant having been overcome and the general peace of 1814 established, they could see no reason why Portugal should have the mortifying role imposed upon it of becoming the colony of an American kingdom; and so, petitions and messages rained down upon the regent, expressing the "ardent desire to see him restored to Lisbon with the royal family." But John's attitude was a stolid one. He would return, yes, but only when "circumstances" permitted it. Napoleon, having been crowned king of the Island of Elba, was still a nightmare and might make it necessary to repeat the flight of 1807.

Even after the Hundred Days, Waterloo, and the imprisonment of the emperor at St. Helena, John remained immovable. It was necessary to consolidate his American monarchy. Dona Carlota Joaquina had received an alarming piece of news: There was a plot afoot to deliver the government of Bahia and Pernambuco into the hands of Bonaparte's brothers, who were then in North America, and in accordance with this plan Napoleon himself was to be "snatched by force from St. Helena." How, then, was he to abandon Brazil in the face of such an emergency as this? Even though incarcerated upon a rock, the emperor of the French did not cease to constitute a menace.

The truth of the matter was that John was becoming extraordinarily attached to his American dominions. He felt himself another man beneath the friendly shade of São Cristovão, or as he threw back his chest and breathed in the air on his Macacos plantation, or along the sunlit highways of Catumbí and Prainha. How could he leave the shores of Guanabara and give up those delightful jaunts to Paquetá? Here he was loved and respected as he had never been before, had no international cares, no frontiers to defend, and was the leading and unchallengeable figure in a world that was wholly new. Under the influence of the virgin soil, his very temperament had been transformed. He had knit his brows and plucked up courage to defy the Corsican, who at that time was humiliating the mightiest sovereigns in Europe. He had afterward invaded Uruguay, despite the opposition of the Holy Alliance, which presumed to determine the geopolitical status quo of colonial possessions. He had put down the Pernambuco revolution of 1817 with an iron fist and had labored with tenacity and energy to prevent the revolt from spreading to other provinces. When he had grown weary of the impertinences of Lord Strangford, all-powerful minister of His Britannic Majesty, he had asked for the envoy's recall with a haughtiness that filled his most intimate counselors with astonishment.

The British government, which had lent wholehearted support to Portuguese aspirations, sought by every means in its power to compel the regent to return to Lisbon. Already in 1813, even before the war had ended, the future George IV, who was then prince regent, had written to John with this purpose in view and had offered to place at his disposition a fleet commanded by Sir John Beresford to aid in transferring the court to the homeland.

John thanked him for his kindness but did not commit himself further. It would not be easy to overcome his reservations and dilatory tactics.

In June, interpreting too freely certain of the monarch's phrases, the British minister had written back to the foreign office, giving them to understand that the moment had come for dispatching Beresford's fleet to Brazil. The British government at once prepared to do so and appointed Canning ambassador to Portugal, with the mission of welcoming the sovereign upon his return.

John was highly indignant at this. What did they mean by making ready the fleet without his orders, when he had not even fixed the date for his departure! Visibly embarrassed, Strangford excused himself by saying that all he had done was to transmit the prince's own wishes so frequently expressed. Out of it all one thing is certain: John was sinking his American roots ever deeper, while Strangford's optimism earned him a severe reprimand from his government. The monarch, apparently, had adopted the New World as his home and was there to stay.

As for the Portuguese, they complained that their ruler only thought of them when he had to recruit soldiers or ask for money. In 1817 he had raised more than 6,000 men for his River Plate campaign, and now he wanted 4,000 more. It was too much! Indeed, he met with such resistance this time that he did not succeed in raising more than 2,900 infantrymen. Then there was the question of money; there was simply not enough to meet all the royal expenditures, such as the sumptuous festivities attendant upon Dom Pedro's wedding, the blockade of Pernambuco, the Montevideo campaign, and other heavy burdens. In view of all this, the wealthy Lusitanians drew in their purse strings. Lend to the government? Not unless they were compelled to do so. In spite of all the guarantees that were offered, John had to resort to force in putting over his loan of 4,000,000 cruzados, in 1817.*

As her husband persisted in his refusal to return to Portugal, Dona Carlota grew desperate. She could no longer endure this horrible climate which was undermining her health. "I have already had five caustics," she wrote to her overseer, João Santos, "and I have been five times to the smoking chamber until I am like a piece of salt meat dried in the sun; and now, cured by the fumes, I am capable of greater resistance, although in this country nothing can resist, nothing lasts, but everything rots." So long as she cherished the hope of obtaining the crown of Spanish America, Dona Carlota bravely put up with the hardships of life in the tropics. There had been four years of intrigues, plottings, and revolutionary manifestoes. At one time it had seemed that everything was in readiness for her to be acclaimed at Buenos Aires as heiress to the rightful kings of Spain who had been incarcerated by Napoleon. At the last moment, however, difficulties had arisen, difficulties created by England and by John himself; and she had been prevented from embarking for the River Plate, thus losing her great opportunity.

Now that her dream had been definitely shattered by the return of her brother, Ferdinand VII, to the Spanish throne in 1814, Dona Carlota could not bear to remain in Brazil any longer. She sent him pathetic appeals, and he wrote to John begging the latter to grant him "the joy and consolation of seeing her once more." He even sent a warship to Rio to bring her back. But John's resources were inexhaustible. He fully agreed to having his wife make the journey but kept putting off her departure so many times that the vessel finally returned to Europe without its precious cargo.

* Approximately $18,000,000 at the present acquisitive power.

In view of John's growing attachment for America, the rumor gained credence that he was urging the nobility to dispose of their European holdings and transfer their wealth to Brazil; but that great syndicate of monarchs, the Holy Alliance, managed by Prince Metternich, soon entered upon the scene. How could they tolerate any longer a vacant throne, leaving the country exposed to the liberal virus that was infecting Europe? The Austrian Chancellor, accordingly, delivered to his special ambassador, Count von Eltz, formal instructions with regard to the pressure that was to be exerted upon the reluctant Braganza. As has been said, the task was no easy one, and John continued to disconcert them all with his evasiveness. Yes, he must return— some day . . . and then he would smile, change the subject, and everything was as it had been before.

The liberal revolution in Spain, which had been unleashed in January of 1820 by the young Rafael de Riego, alarmed all Europe; and Portugal, by reason of its proximity, was not long in feeling the results of it. The English marshal Beresford, who was the true if uncrowned king of Portugal, was the only one to foresee the course of events. He had called in vain for a force of 6,000 men to help Ferdinand VII maintain his absolute sovereignty; and now, with the house next door on fire, it was hard to keep the flame from spreading. There was but one thing to do, and that was to cross the Atlantic and undertake to persuade the king to return at once in order to avert the crisis. On February 4, 1820, he set sail for Brazil on the frigate *Spartan*.

John gave signs of sorrow upon receiving the bad news, but when the marshal suggested that the sovereign and his heir should go back to Portugal without delay, the former turned a deaf ear and ended by entrusting the visitor with the task of inspecting and reorganizing the Brazilian army and its military establishments, such as hospitals and depots. Finally, in view of the pressure brought to bear by the British envoy, who had received very precise instructions from Wellington, he decided that the situation might be adequately met if Beresford were to return with a little money and many promises; and with this idea in mind he turned over to the marshal more than 100,000 duros * with which to pay off the troops. He then sent him back on the *Vengeur*.

But it was too late. The revolution of Oporto, launched on August 24, 1820, had been successful and Beresford was unable even to land. The ancient monarchical Cortes had been convoked by the rebels, a measure that properly could emanate only from the king; yet John lacked the courage to outlaw those responsible for this subversive movement. With a simulation of dignity, he mildly condemned the act; but inasmuch as the parliamentary body was already functioning, let it present the king with the results of its deliberations for his sanction. If everything turned out satisfactorily, John promised them as a reward, the Portuguese should have as their European ruler either his own royal person or one of his sons or descendants, since it was necessary that some member of the royal family remain in Brazil "for the consolidation, union, and reciprocal advantage of the united kingdom." Who was this "someone" to be, father or son?

Meanwhile, in high government circles at Rio, a veritable battle was taking place between the foreign minister, Count Palmela, an aristocrat with enlightened ideas whose contacts with the courts and peoples of the Old World had taught him the magnitude of events taking place in the early years of the century, and Thomaz Antônio, an influential favorite for whom Portuguese liberalism meant nothing more than "a case for the police, and more police." Palmela counseled his sovereign to consent to a constitutional monarchy after the English model and to

* Approximately $50,000.

send the crown prince to Portugal to govern that country and oversee the drawing up of a constitution. "There is not a moment to be lost," he said; "firm and decisive measures must be adopted, and such as are suited to the temper of the times."

To this Thomaz Antônio replied: "My opinion is the direct opposite of the one that has just been stated. Your Majesty should not bow to the revolutionaries nor permit the scepter to slip from your grasp. This madness cannot last for long, and when it is past it is essential that you should be a king and not a president." A passionate argument ensued in which a number of persons took part, among them the crown prince, the queen, Silvestre Pinheiro, João Severiano, the count of Arcos, and other Portuguese leaders. After much discussion they finally reached an agreement, each one yielding "the half of his own opinion." In place of the father, the son should go.

Brazil, with its deeply rooted liberal and semirepublican traditions, was to be profoundly stirred by the uprising of Oporto. The first news of the event had at once inflamed the settlements of Pará and other ports of northeastern Brazil. Fraternizing together, the people and the soldiery gathered in the public squares to acclaim the victory of liberal and constitutional ideas, and by February 17th (1821) Rio had received news of the proclamation of a constitutional regime in Bahia. Then it was that the colorful figure of the crown prince came into prominence. He brought with him into ministerial councils the agitation of the streets, taverns, and secret societies. He was conscious of the nearing storm but was not disturbed by it; the novelty of the situation appealed to him as well as the opportunity that was afforded him of observing events, forming his own opinions, seating himself at the council table and—making himself heard.

Palmela hastily drew up a manifesto containing the bases of

a constitution, but the king, influenced by Thomaz Antônio, preferred to adopt a more prudent formula and merely issued a proclamation convoking a similar Cortes in Rio de Janeiro for the purpose of adapting to local needs the provisions of the constitution that was to be voted in Lisbon. The kingdom it seemed was to have two constitutions and two capitals, the latter to be inhabited alternately by the sovereign and the crown prince. In this manner, even though the Portuguese constitution might succeed in despoiling him of all his prerogatives as an absolute monarch, in Brazil, at least, he might still preserve a few of them.

Popular reaction was not slow in coming; the young prince had been right about that. The street corners were soon plastered with violent placards and pasquinades, advocating in unbridled terms the immediate adoption of the entire constitution as drawn up in Portugal; and on the morning of February 26th, the soldiery, spurred on by agitators, appeared drawn up in military formation in the public square. Their attitude was a threatening one; but John was to show himself to be indeed a cautious individual, for when a friar came to wake him on that tumultuous morning, the sovereign, still dazed with sleep, rubbed his eyes, sent for Dom Pedro, and ordered the prince to go at once to Thomaz Antônio's house and procure the decree "which had been drawn up the night before for just such an emergency as this."

There was no coup that could take him by surprise; he always had prepared, well in advance, the infallible countermeasure. He now dispatched the crown prince to the square, bearing the decree and panting with enthusiasm at having been elevated to so important a role in the events that were taking place. Carretti's soldiers cheered him as he rode up on the gallop, and he, with great decisiveness of bearing, then turned to the close-packed, howling mob that stood there among the gun carriages and stacked-up muskets. "Why all this commotion," he exclaimed, "when everything has already been attended to?" With this he waved the decree (which had been predated the 24th) that announced John's adherence to the constitution that was being prepared by the Cortes of Lisbon. "The troops," he concluded, "may now retire to their barracks and the officers may go kiss the hand of my august Father."

But this was not the end of the matter. Macamboa, leader of the faction, returned to the rostrum and thundered: in addition to an oath of loyalty to the constitution, the people demanded the appointment of new ministers and other high functionaries. Dom Pedro did not waver. Leaping expertly into the saddle, he cracked his whip and made off for São Cristovão to consult the king. With no means of resisting, John agreed to everything. He would let the revolutionary wave spend itself, and afterward he would be able to restore the royal authority. Returning to the square, the prince summoned the city magistrates and, along with Dom Miguel, the soldiers, and the people, took the oath of allegiance to the constitution, an oath administered by the court chaplain. He then read the decree in which the king consented to all the people's demands, guaranteed freedom of opinion, and announced the removal of the ministers. With emphasis he repeated the names of the new authorities. Mad with enthusiasm, the populace cheered the sovereign and began calling for the "illustrious and magnanimous Braganza." The king! The king! was the cry that went up.

Digging his spurs into his jaded steed, the indefatigable Pedro forthwith returned to São Cristovão to bring his father. Stretching his shaky limbs, John adjusted his three-cornered plumed hat and, deeply moved by it all, entered his carriage. "To the square!" they shouted to the postilion; and in this manner they set out, with the prince, very proud of himself, riding alongside and keeping a watchful eye on the drowsy monarch, whose stout person

loaded down the ancient coach. It was around eleven o'clock when
the carriage appeared in the square, whereupon the unruly crowd
burst into a tremendous ovation. Removing the horses from the
shafts, they themselves hauled the carriage and began a triumphal
march to the palace through the rua do Ouvidor, which was over-
flowing with spectators.

That night at the theater there was a gala performance of
Rossini's light opera, *La Cenerentola*. Rubbing his hairy hands
together, John smiled: all this enthusiasm over a bit of paper divided into articles and paragraphs. . . . The following day,
in conversing with the Austrian minister Stürmer, he wittily
commented on the episode: "Doesn't it strike you as humorous,
forcing someone to swear to a thing that does not exist and may
never come into existence?"

At four o'clock on the afternoon of April 20th, the electors
of the parish of Rio de Janeiro gathered in the Bourse, in the
rua do Sabão. It was the desire of Silvestre Pinheiro, John's
minister, to have the assembly take some broad action to consolidate the country's institutions, and to have it declare itself
opposed to the monarch's return to Portugal, for he had finally
resolved to embark; but everything turned out just the opposite.
Having arbitrarily declared itself a national convention, that
body was seized with a violent revolutionary fever. When the
president went to read Silvestre Pinheiro's message of advice and
the decree instituting Dom Pedro's regency, the first signs of
irreverence and lack of discipline were manifested in the
auditorium. From high up on the benches some of the electors
bawled: "Louder! Read louder! We can't hear a word!" And the
venerable magistrate had to turn over the reading of the documents to a stentorian-voiced individual perched on "one of the
most prominent seats." His timidity still further excited the

audacity of the crowd that packed the galleries and insisted upon taking a part in the discussion. It proved to be impossible to read the instructions regarding the functioning of the regency (it had been decided, also, that Dom Pedro was to remain in Brazil) or the list of newly appointed state secretaries.

"None of that!" shouted the galleries. "We want the Spanish constitution until the Portuguese one has been drafted. No more ministers appointed by the king. Only the people has the right to name them."

Thoroughly aroused, the leaders of the various groups began invading the enclosure reserved for the electors and even went up to the president's table, where they proceeded to impose upon the tremulous magistrate the will of the mob. The shouting reached a climax when someone scrawled on a column the words: "The grateful nation calls for the Count of Arcos." The galleries howled at this: "No grandees! We don't want that poser!" And then, little by little, four men came to assume absolute control of the gathering: a priest, a merchant, a surgeon commonly known as "Cavaquinho" (Mandolin), and a youth of twenty who was the son of a French tailor.

With this there occurred one of those curious and fleeting phenomena that are produced as a result of crowd psychology and that are ended by mere chance. At given moments of history, moments of crisis, confusion, or tragedy, unlooked-for figures suddenly arise to play a leading part and then are gone in an instantaneous flash, to be lost in the darkness out of which they came, the whole thing taking place as if by a magician's trick or as a formidable joke of some kind. In such a manner this youth of twenty, this tailor's son, was to flash across the pages of Brazilian history. Tall, lean, long-faced, with brown eyes and blond hair, Luiz Duprat that afternoon wore a gingham jacket, a black silk vest, and nankeen trousers. It was the first time he had spoken in public, but he excelled them all in vehemence and enthusiasm. Gesticulating and shouting "like one possessed," to quote the words of an eyewitness, he made himself the real dictator of the convention and ended by swaying the entire junta, the members of which were thoroughly terrified. "When he wished to emphasize his points, he leaped the railing that separated the people from the delegates and came all the way up to the table." He declared that he had no confidence in the government. The people had been deceived by the pretended changes of the 26th of February. What they wanted now was the Spanish constitution, "the noblest work of the human mind."

They accordingly proceeded to appoint a committee to "request" the king to proclaim the adoption of the constitution in question. It was pouring rain when the delegates left the hall for the city palace. John was not there, and so they at once set out for São Cristovão, where the sovereign received them in the company of Dom Pedro, Silvestre Pinheiro, and the ministers of the interior and of the navy. As on the 26th of February, the monarch once more gave his consent. To be sure, he would accept the Spanish constitution or any other. Was it not, like the Portuguese one, a mere scrap of paper divided into articles and paragraphs? But Dom Pedro felt that the moment had come to act with the greatest of energy. He did no talking but sent out and had a battalion of chasseurs and a detachment of artillery assembled there on the estate. The ruffians of Commerce Square were going to find at last that they had a man to deal with.

The news speedily reached the assembly, which, in a state of great excitement, appointed another committee to demand an explanation of the king. Having suddenly become the spokesman of the people, young Duprat decreed that the military governor must appear before him within an hour at the most, and when Brigadier General Caula arrived, this son of a French tailor addressed him as one would a subordinate. The people had gone mad with power, and a twenty-year-old lad was threatening to overthrow the Portuguese monarchy. Led by Duprat, the assembly passed a decree to the effect that John was not to leave the country carrying away the people's money, and the fortresses were ordered to close the harbor "under pain of death." No ship was to be allowed to pass, "from a fishing smack to the largest vessel." The regime was going to pieces and the authorities and the army were capitulating before a handful of nobodies. They were not going to permit the Braganza to depart with shiploads of gold. With his fists in the air, Duprat screamed: "The law that says money shall not be taken out of the country has not been revoked!" And the crowd in the streets, leaping with joy, proceeded to make up a song:

> With eyes alert and footstep bold,
> We'll go on board and get the gold.

When the second delegation from the assembly arrived at the palace demanding to know why it was that troops had been concentrated upon the estate, Dom Pedro's laconic answer was, "You will see!" And, losing no time, he ordered that the assembly be dissolved by fair means or foul. The troops then marched down to the square, and from there proceeded to the rua Direita and the Mineiros Quay. At the entrance to the rua do Sabão a company of the third battalion of infantry was stationed with two pieces of artillery in order to dominate the entrance of the building.

It was four o'clock in the morning. His men having fired into the air, the company commander, Major Peixoto, with a few soldiers made his way inside with the object of breaking up the meeting. He was greeted by a bullet which, however, left him unscathed. He then ordered his men to fix bayonets and charge the seditious multitude. The door was broken down and the place cleared with rifle butts in the course of a few minutes. Many in their terror leaped out of windows and cast themselves into the sea. A number of the dead and wounded and a few prisoners, including Duprat, were taken to Snake Island. The storm had passed, but the monarchy, rocked by the shouts of that "bedeviled" youth, was still trembling down to its foundations.

These events in Rio led John to make up his mind at last to return to Europe, leaving Pedro as the regent and viceroy of Portuguese America. At nightfall of April 24th, the king embarked, and on the 26th he crossed the harbor bar followed by two frigates and nine transports, accompanied by three thousand persons, and carrying with him 50,000,000 cruzados.* To Silvestre Pinheiro, the one minister who had voted against his leaving, the monarch at the last moment voiced the lament: "To think it has come to this! We were defeated!" But on the way, he naïvely discovered one ray of hope. Supposing they were to put in at Bahia? The residents of that city might oblige him to stay. . . . But this was out of the question; the fleet was already making for the mouth of the Tagus. The king heaved a deep sigh, and Dona Carlota gave a smile that afforded a glimpse of her decaying teeth.

* Approximately $250,000,000 at the present rate.

CHAPTER SIX

"INDEPENDENCE OR DEATH!"

John left the government of the enormous country entirely to the discretion of the twenty-two-year-old prince. Upon the latter fell the task of appointing and dismissing ministers, administering justice, handling finances, commuting or pardoning death sentences, making war and concluding peace, and conferring honors and decorations. Knight-errant of the ideal, prizing glory more than life itself and honor above everything else, Dom Pedro was to flash across the sky of history like a turbulent meteor, astounding, perplexing, and alarming all beholders with the contradictions of his character. He was to live without restraint of any kind, giving way to every impulse, good or bad, at any time, and acting without reservations, subterfuge, or ulterior motives. Uncontrollably emotional, he was easily moved to tears and stirred by human frailties. He was harsh at times but never cruel, and the sight of a child could arouse all his tenderness. On the other hand, he was passionately fond of danger; and confronting an enemy, sword in hand, he did not pause to measure his foeman's strength before exposing his own bosom to the thrust.

His life was to be a broad and generous improvisation guided solely by instinct. He was lacking in the culture suited to a prince and without formal training, yet one of the first things he did upon assuming the regency of Brazil was to lift the customs duty on foreign books and abolish the censorship which previously had existed in connection with everything that appeared in print. He then went on to order the adoption of the Lancaster method in the primary grades and provided for the opening of law courses at São Paulo and Olinda; at the same time he set the most distinguished historians to work upon the chronicles of the empire and saw to the reprinting of works of general or scientific interest and the founding of a medical society, an astronomical observatory, and educational institutions of every grade.

The blood of tyrants ran in his veins, yet his only thought was of liberty, even though in struggling for it he sometimes did it violence. His respect for the rights of others was admirable, seeing that he came of a line of absolute monarchs who had ruled for seven centuries. To the mistress who had come to dominate his heart he was to write: "Ask of me what you will so long as it does no harm to any other."

The situation of Brazil at the beginning of 1821 was extremely delicate and uncertain. Finances were in a state of collapse and the distant provinces of the north, having no ties that bound them to the capital, were threatening to separate and refuse to acknowledge the regent's authority. The seriousness and composure with which the youth took over the task of governing surprised even his most intimate friends and counselors. Before cutting the salaries and pensions of state functionaries, which was one of his first measures of economy, he reduced by half his own allowance. He then plunged into the administrative tasks that awaited him. He did away with the duty on salt to benefit the cattle-raising and fishing industries, and adopted a measure guaranteeing property owners against expropriation. Rendering effective the freedom of the individual, he proceeded to abolish dungeons, forced labor, irons, and flogging for prisoners, observing that penal institutions were intended "for the detention of persons and not for flagellating them or undermining their health."

Between five and six in the morning he was up and around and at once went out to inspect the barracks and government offices, to oversee the arrival of functionaries and interrogate them, and to lead the troops in their exercises as he pointed out short-comings and examined their equipment. He had breakfast at nine and dinner at two, spending not more than twenty minutes on either meal. Between breakfast and the siesta hour he saw his ministers and transacted affairs of state. At four he generally went for an outing, on horseback or in his carriage, alone or with his consort. At twilight he would play the flute, accompanied by his princess on the piano, and at nine he would calmly go to sleep —when he did not slip quietly out of the house to pursue his amours.[1] On Fridays he held public audience, settling all questions with great ability. Those petitions that were not disposed of immediately were sure to be attended to within the next three days. The administrative machinery now began moving, impelled by a sovereign who personally went through his functionaries' files and threatened with prosecution those guilty of obstructing the work of government.

Extremely sensitive and emotional, as has been said, he made no attempt at self-control. In São Paulo on one occasion, among those who appeared to greet him was a septuagenarian who looked as if he had been dug up out of the past. Clad in a blood-red greatcoat, a ruffled shirt, and a black cocked hat, and wearing his hair done up in beribboned curls, the patriarch Vicente Taques Góes e Aranha, poet and Latinist and governor of the town of Itú since 1779, with his fancy dress and his fossilized dignity drew from Dom Pedro a loud guffaw. Deeply wounded, the old man retired to nurse his sorrow, but the prince at once repented and sent for him to repair the wrong that had been done, with many proofs of his consideration. Months later he made him a knight of the Order of the Southern Cross, and sometime afterward conferred upon him the Medal of Christ.[2]

A similar episode occurred in connection with a rich land-owner of Minas who was famed for his large fortune and small stature. When Dom Pedro inquired his name, he replied with a radiant smile: "João Baptista Ferreira de Souza Coutinho." The prince, unable to contain himself, laughed in the man's face: "Why, your name is bigger than you are!" This witticism won for the victim the title of Baron of Catas Altas, while the imperial jester received in return a dinner service of gold plate.[3]

Dissimulation and disloyalty had no part in Pedro's make-up. In 1823, when he had dissolved the Constituent Assembly and ordered the deportation of the principal opposition leaders, certain persons of influence in the palace conceived the clever idea of diverting from its course the ship bearing the exiles in order that the latter might be taken prisoner in Portuguese waters; the apostolic faction, which then held absolute sway over the government in Lisbon, would see to the rest. . . . The commandant who was looked upon as being the man to carry out this mission confided the astute plan to Dom Pedro. "If Your Majesty will consent to it, I promise to see that it is done in such a way as to spare us all any responsibility in the matter." Dom Pedro, far from being pleased with such a scheme for conveniently doing away with his bitterest enemies, rose to his feet in energetic protest: "No! I will not give my consent, for that would be an act of treachery."

This prince who had been known to flog dishonest functionaries, who spoke his mind freely and often violently to British diplomats, and who crushed his enemies with his own hands, once apologized in public to a steward whom he had unjustly offended. As Pedro was about to enter the residence of one of his mistresses, the guardian of the wardrobe who accompanied him, José de Andrade Pinto, stopped short and boldly refused to go any further.

"Upon the threshold of this doorway my functions end," he said.

"Very well, then," was Dom Pedro's furious retort, "you may consider yourself dismissed from my service." But on the following day he sent for the rebellious attendant. "Just forget that I said it; I have thought it over, and you only did your duty."

The attraction that he felt for the fair sex was one of his most typical characteristics. At every period of his life we come upon traces of his amorous adventures, stimulated by the tropical climate and his own exuberant sensuality. While he was still but a lad, many fathers had taken precautions against his incursions upon their daughters. One of them had met him at the entrance to the house, where he stopped the prince, saying: "Senhor Dom Miguel may enter, for he is a child; but Your Highness, being a man, may not, for people's tongues are already beginning to wag." Before his marriage Pedro had been fond of the company of the French dancers and modistes who were then the sensation of the town; and three months after Leopoldina's arrival, the ballerina Noemí Valençay, whom John had hastily packed off to Pernambuco, gave birth to a bastard whose father was the prince.

An affair with more serious consequences was one that occurred in 1822. The lady in this case was Clémence Saisset, also French, who was married to the proprietor of a fashionable dress shop in the rua do Ouvidor. Dom Pedro was in the habit of visiting her at her home, in the daytime and quite openly, without being in the least concerned with the feelings of her husband, who was but a "super" in this bit of vaudeville. By way of compensation, the firm was authorized to put up the imperial arms in front of the shop and as a result found the means of paying off its debts. But as Dom Pedro grew more excessive in his liberality, the public clamor against the ménage increased; and one day, when the prince was out of the city, a bullet was fired through the Frenchman's window, whereupon he, thoroughly terrified, went to seek the protection of the minister Gestas, who made a report setting forth the episode in minute detail. Some days later the pair embarked for Europe, but not before they had received from Dom Pedro's agent a check against Rothschild's for 73,000 francs and an additional 6,000 francs in gold. Madame Saisset carried in her arms a ten-months-old infant, Pedro de Alcântara Brasileiro, who later in France was to display an impulsiveness which he had inherited from his father.

A royal Lovelace, Dom Pedro was to leave behind him a long and varied record of amours, some of them well vouched for while others are veiled in obscurity or else are purely imaginary; but in any case, if a complete list of those attributed to him were drawn up, it would be an interminable one. In that list would be found: the wife of General Jorge de Avilez, commander of the Portuguese garrison at Rio; the witty Senhora Bonpland, married to that hunter of rare plants, the French naturalist Aimé Bonpland; Anna Steinhausen, wife of Leopoldina's librarian; Madame de Saturville, who was married to a rich jewel merchant; the Uruguayan Carmen García; Maria Joana Sodré; Joana Mosqueira, the mulatto; the Baroness of Sorocaba— How many others?

The Portuguese liberals, having won the first of their demands, which was that John should return to Lisbon, were now revealing clearly their design to reduce Brazil once more to the status of a colony by abolishing those rights and privileges that had been granted it by the monarch. Practically a prisoner of the

Cortes, the sovereign could do nothing to prevent the enactment of laws that inspired the greatest discontent among Brazilians and incited them to revolt. This external factor was to work a miracle within the country by uniting its inhabitants everywhere, even in the most remote provinces, around the separatist movement. It was not merely political instinct, but rather a feeling of complete identification with the new land—Portugal being for him no more than a vague and distant memory—that led the regent cleverly to prepare for independence by anticipating the will of the people, who otherwise would have achieved it in opposition to the monarchy.

King John, with his keen political insight, had foreseen with extraordinary accuracy the course that events were to take. Two days before leaving for Portugal, he had confided to his son: "If Brazil should decide on separation, let it be under your leadership, since you are bound to respect me, rather than under that of one of these adventurers." Acting from constraint, and trembling for his very life, John now saw himself forced to accept those decrees of the Cortes that were aimed at destroying the work that he had accomplished in America during all these years and that gave promise of being so fruitful in its results. Secretly, however, outwitting the stern censorship that surrounded him, he urged his son to resist and so preserve Brazil—that masterpiece of a dynasty—from revolt and dissolution.

Dom Pedro, meanwhile, had to watch his step, for there was a strong military force, known as the Legion and commanded by General Jorge de Avilez, in the heart of Rio de Janeiro. On June 5th, as if to assert its authority, this detachment staged an uprising and compelled the regent not only to set up a governing junta charged with the task of examining all proposed legislation, but also to send into exile the Count of Arcos, his principal minister, who was accused of being an enemy of the Cortes. This was a crucial moment for Dom Pedro. Although he lacked the armed strength to silence the impertinent legionnaires, his first impulse was to assemble a couple of Brazilian battalions and hurl himself into the fight against this odious supervision which the Portuguese had made him accept. Things did not go so far, however. Barely able to resist making a rash move, Pedro yielded for the moment, exiled his friend, and set up the junta; but to his intimates he stated that it was only for the good of the people that he had done so and that his enemies had best not attempt to force such a sacrifice upon him again, or "God only knows what will happen."

This compromise weakened his royal authority but saved the cause of Brazilian nationalism from being stamped out. Deceived by his action, the Legion quieted down and the prince was able to gain time and prepare for its ultimate annihilation. Discovering in Pedro a potential enemy whose separatist tendencies were already clearly revealed, the Cortes decided that he must return to Europe immediately, the excuse being that he ought to visit the principal countries of that Continent in order better to prepare himself for the task of reigning. This order, drawn up in terms that were too imperious, naturally wounded his sensibilities and alarmed the Brazilians, who saw in it a decisive step toward the total recolonization of Brazil. In all the provinces Masonic lodges were urging the people to resist the decrees of the Cortes. The prince dispatched emissaries to the principal centers to sound out the temper of the inhabitants, and the results were surprising. Petitions, manifestoes, and appeals poured in upon him bearing thousands of signatures. It was a true plebiscite, calling upon him not to abandon the country.

On the 9th of January, in the presence of a wildly cheering multitude, the regent in his city palace received the dramatic manifesto presented to him by the people of Rio de Janeiro. The document was read by the president of the city council and stressed the point that, if the prince were to leave, anarchy would rule the land and the unity of the kingdom would be destroyed. Firmly and serenely—for his frightened ministers had deserted him—Pedro replied: "Inasmuch as it is for the good of all and the general well-being of the nation, I hereby consent; you may say to the people that I am remaining here." *Fico* (I am staying)—that word was to become a historic one. Transmitted to the people, it provoked a riotous outburst of enthusiasm. The prince now was not merely holding out against the Portuguese Cortes; he was publicly defying it, repudiating its tutelage, and tearing up its decrees. This was open revolt, nothing less.

The Portuguese garrison now rose in arms and prepared to put the prince on board a ship and take him back to Lisbon by force. Having hurried his family off to Santa Cruz—his first born now three years old and his princess, who was in the eighth month of another pregnancy—Pedro hastily mobilized his forces for the struggle. At Campo de Santana various infantry and artillery units were concentrated, and these were joined by numerous popular contingents armed with pistols, knives, and cudgels, while in their ranks were numerous priests and friars grasping ancient blunderbusses. Occupying the neighboring heights, the Portuguese with their cannon might have dispersed this army of patriots, but while their commander was hesitating to fire upon the heir to the crown, his future king, the latter was engaged in consolidating his troops, with the result that the enemy had to retire to Praia Grande on the other side of the bay, in order to keep from being surrounded. The prince then sent word that they should embark at once for Portugal, and when they declined to do so, he dispatched General Curado to hem them in by land and commanded his warships to block their passage by sea.

Being solidly entrenched, the Portuguese declared that they would only embark when fresh troops arrived from Europe to relieve them. This was precisely what Dom Pedro feared; once the Legion was reenforced with fresh regiments, he would not possess the means of dealing with it. He must precipitate events, which he did by sending the legionnaires a violent ultimatum to the effect that if they did not embark at once he would crush them with fire and sword within a few hours' time. There was nothing for the Portuguese to do but capitulate; for Pedro, having fortified the wharves with artillery and occupied the fortresses of Santa Cruz and Pico, was only awaiting the arrival of contingents that were speeding to him from Minas and São Paulo. On the 15th of February, escorted by two Brazilian ships, the transports put out to sea bearing the vanquished troops. The king of Portugal's soldiers having been expelled, the land was now practically emancipated. To a minister of state whose absence he had noted in the moment of danger and who inquired where their next official meeting was to take place, whether in the city or in São Cristovão, he coldly replied: "Neither here nor there."

It was precisely at this period, as he was enjoying the glorious privilege of founding an American dynasty, that another people, the Greeks, turned to the young prince and offered him the crown of their country. Ever since the year before, they had been carrying on an insurrection against the tyrannical yoke of the Turks; and in spite of the tremendous reprisals exacted by the armies of Mahmud II, the Hellenic cities had been occupied, one after another, by the patriots. The Ottomans had been surrounded on the Acropolis, Epirus had been liberated, and at the pass of Thermopylae the epic stand of Leonidas had been repeated; the Turkish fleet sent against Samos had been wiped out, and the first national assembly had met solemnly to proclaim the nation's independence and adopt a temporary constitution.

In the west, notwithstanding warm manifestations of sympathy on the part of the peoples, the governments had maintained a reserved and even hostile attitude toward the movement. The chief thing that Metternich, the leading figure in European politics, perceived in the Greek struggle for independence was a rebellion against the sultan's lawfully constituted authority. For this reason he saw to it that at Laybach the Greek delegates who had been sent to ask for aid were not even received. Public opinion, however, contrasted strongly with the official attitude of the powers; for Europe had been electrified by the heroism of the revolutionists, and volunteers from every country had followed the example of Byron, who gave his life for the cause of freedom, and of Colonel Favier, who organized and commanded the first regular troops in the peninsula. In the same way, many others were ready to embark upon this new crusade, the object of which was to save the illustrious birthplace of Occidental culture.

In April, 1822, the sultan's great punitive expedition disembarked in Chios and laid waste the island with terrible ferocity. Of the 90,000 inhabitants, 23,000 were massacred and nearly 50,000 women and children were sold as slaves. Andreas Miaulis, however, reorganized the Greek fleet, and with incredible daring succeeded in routing the Turks, slaying their leader and more than 3,000 men. On the 16th of April, a Greek envoy, Captain Nicolau Chiefala Greco, solicited an audience with the king of Portugal, John VI, in order to offer the latter's son the sovereign crown of Greece.[4]

Convinced that Pedro's residence in Brazil meant the inevitable separation of the colony, the Lisbon Cortes saw in this offer of the Greek throne a providential means of assuring the prince's return. Deeply flattered, Dom Pedro would surely accept such a

distinction and embark for Europe upon the first ship. Between
the two countries there could not be the slightest hesitation on
his part. How compare Greece to Brazil, which was no more than
a far-off colony, peopled with colored races and without any conveniences or civilization? And once this had been effected, a
military expedition could be sent to Brazil without any further
delay and the desired recolonization of the country could be undertaken with every likelihood of success.

But Dom Pedro was indissolubly bound to the new land in
whose womb (so instinct whispered to him) a new and wonderful civilization was germinating. The journey to Vila Rica had
given him some idea of the extent of his dominions—you could
put the whole of Europe within the frontiers of Brazil; and contact with the laborious and enthusiastic inhabitants of the interior
had convinced him that it was here in America that the future
was being built as Europe went down in the throes of revolution
and Asia continued to labor under the burden of millenniums of
history. No, he would not betray the hopes that the Brazilians
had placed in him. Were they not ready to acclaim him as their
"Perpetual Defender"? He would not give in to the vanity that
went with wearing the diadem of the country that was the fatherland of Homer and Pericles. Instead, with even greater pride, he
would stick a green coffee branch into his soldier's helmet as a
symbol of the new imperial springtime that was bursting into
bloom.

He carefully kept his father informed of the dizzying course
of events: the formation of a new cabinet chosen from among
Brazilians; the creation of a council of state; the pacification of
Minas Gerais; the conferring of the title "Perpetual Defender of
Brazil"; and the convocation of a constituent assembly. He was
ardent and vociferous in expressing his opinion of the Portuguese

Cortes: "I say to that bloodthirsty mob that I, as Prince Regent of Brazil and its Perpetual Defender, mean to declare null and void all the decrees of those stinking and pestiferous Machiavellian troublemakers, and that those decrees will not be carried out." And further on: "If this frank declaration should irritate those Lusitanian-Spaniards, let them send an army against us, and we will show them what Brazilian valor is."

At Bahia, General Madeira was in command of the Portuguese reactionaries; and he now fortified himself in São Salvador, where he held out for twelve months. The Brazilians, meanwhile, were organizing to fight him, and Dom Pedro wrote to his father: "I mean to put him out; if necessary, I will starve him out!" The governing Junta of Minas Gerais having refused to recognize the prince's authority, he decided to go and subdue that province in person. Accompanied only by a small escort, he began the journey to Vila Rica, the provincial capital and center of the up-rising. When he was about halfway there, he was met by some of the local authorities who were loyal to him and who had come to warn him of the danger to his life should he go on to that city. They informed him that a state of great excitement prevailed in the town and that the officials were determined to prevent him from entering.

Dom Pedro smiled and spurred on his mount harder than ever, being eager to put down the revolt with his own hands. Wherever he passed, the people came out to acclaim him and promise him obedience. By the time he reached Capão da Lama, he already had under his command four regiments of militia. As he approached the city, two members of the junta came out to render homage to him, but Pedro repelled them curtly, saying, "It is a bit late," and urged his tired steed onward. He came up to the gates of the city accompanied only by a few civilians with not one soldier among them, and this exhibition of courage completely disarmed his adversaries and won for him the enthusiastic support of the people, who applauded him deliriously. He thereupon removed those of the authorities who had been implicated in the revolt, summoned the electors to choose another junta, and turned over the military command to an officer whom he trusted.

With this expedition to Vila Rica, the prince began a series of journeys that were to render him famous for the extraordinary speed with which he covered enormous distances as he rode on with scarcely any rest at all, leaving far behind him his exhausted escorts. His return to Rio de Janeiro established a notable record for that era: setting out from Vila Rica on April 21 (1822), he arrived at the capital of the kingdom at eight o'clock on the night of the 25th, having covered in that time a distance of eighty leagues.* Going directly to the theater, where a gala evening was in progress, he threw back the curtains of the royal box and proudly addressed the awed occupants of the orchestra seats, who had supposed that he was still many miles away: "I have come from Vila Rica in four days and a half. Everything is tranquil there!" His last words were drowned out in a tremendous burst of applause. His auditors did not know which to praise the more: the result of the mission or the young regent's astonishing ride.

The French minister Maler, overcome with admiration, wrote home to his government: "He rode eighty leagues in less than five days. He has been in the saddle for thirty days, and yet fatigue does not seem to have impaired his bounding health!"

Disorders having broken out in São Paulo, Pedro once again decided to go and settle matters himself. On August 14, 1822, accompanied only by a secretary, two servants, the Lieutenant Canto e Melo, and his inseparable crony Chalaça, he entered upon a journey that was to have such consequences for his own

* About 320 miles.

private life and for the future of Brazil as he would never have
been able to foresee. His entrance into the city of São Paulo,
capital of the province, was as triumphal as the one at Vila Rica
had been. Fireworks, salvos of artillery, and the clanging of bells
greeted the arrival of the prince, who made a deep impression on
the people as he rode through the crowded streets mounted on
his handsome charger with the silver trappings, the very per-
sonification of martial elegance.

On September 7th, returning to São Paulo from a brief visit
to Santos on the seaboard, he was galloping briskly along when
he was stopped by a couple of gentlemen on horseback, one of
whom he at once recognized as a court messenger, Paulo Bregaro.
Breathlessly, the messenger drew from his pouch two letters, one
from the princess and the other from José Bonifácio, known to
history as the "patriarch of independence." Dom Pedro read both
communications with avidity and frowned severely at the news
they contained: the Portuguese government was making ready
a huge expedition for the definitive subjugation of Brazil; and at
Bahia, last center of resistance, Madeira's forces were plucking
up fresh courage at the prospect of such powerful reenforcements.
At once the prince realized that the moment had come to make
his supreme decision. The Cortes would never be able to understand his sincere desire to assure, to the best of his ability, the
unity of the realm. They were treating him as an enemy and
were preparing to make war upon him. Slender-looking in his
blue cavalryman's uniform, he grasped the hilt of his sword. It
was half-past four in the afternoon and the sun was shining gently
down. So, he thought, the Cortes wanted war; they should have
it!

"Off with these emblems, soldiers!" he cried, snatching the
Portuguese colors from his uniform and hurling them to the
ground. Even as they fell, one by one, he unsheathed his sword

and raised it high in the air: "By the blood that flows in my veins and upon my honor I swear to God to free Brazil!"

A unanimous cry went up that echoed over the green fields of Ypiranga: "We swear it!" The scene was an impressive one, vigorous and colorful, with the naked swords of the guard of honor glistening in the sunlight as the civilians, heads bared and overcome with emotion, kept their eyes fixed upon their prince who now rose in the stirrups and shouted:

"Independence or death!"

This shout having been repeated by the guard, they all enthusiastically trooped back to the city. The news spread as if by magic, occasioning the wildest demonstrations in front of the palace, where the prince was busy designing an armband with the motto "Independence or Death," to be exhibited at the theater that evening, and composing an anthem which three hours and a half later was to thrill the São Paulo populace:

> Arise, ye noble citizens,
> Cast out all fear for good or ill,
> For our brave bosoms and our arms
> Shall be the walls that guard Brazil.

It was not enough for him to have given the country its independence, he must provide its hymn as well, and he himself must sing it in the royal box that night, echoed by the rhetorical transports of the Paulistas in prose and verse.

Dom Pedro at that moment was the incarnation of a collective soul-state. Therein lies his principal merit. He had sensed the aspirations of the people that he governed and had allied himself to his country's destiny in place of vainly opposing a movement that could not be put down. But there was something else that happened to the young prince during these days that seemed too momentous to permit of any other emotions than those that had to do with the liberation of Brazil. In the suburbs of São Paulo his eyes encountered those of the woman who was to hold him enslaved forever after. Domitila de Castro Canto e Melo was the name of the one whom fate had placed in Dom Pedro's path; and the background of their first meeting was the scene that had witnessed the birth of the Brazilian Empire.

CHAPTER SEVEN

THE "BRAZILIAN POMPADOUR" AND THE
BIRTH OF AN EMPIRE

It was the singular destiny of women of the Castro family to inspire love in regal bosoms. Pedro I of Castile had let himself become hopelessly ensnared by the charms of Dona Joana de Castro, and their scandalous affair had deeply shocked the Spanish court. Later, Dona Inês de Castro was to inspire in another Pedro, the first Portuguese monarch of that name, one of the greatest passions in history. When she was struck down by a dagger thrust inspired by those who feared her baleful influence upon the dynasty, her royal lover went mad, tore out the hearts of her assassins with his own hands, drank their warm blood with a savage snarl, and stunned his courtiers and the world, and gave vent to his own hatred and despair, by having his mistress, even as she lay there cold in death, crowned queen of Portugal.

The years went by and a capricious fate rekindled in the breasts of the grandson and granddaughter of this pair the same all-consuming flame. It is the year 1822—a tropical background this time, with perfumed breezes blowing—and a group of Negro slaves are vainly endeavoring to ford a stream bearing a litter that conceals a beautiful lady. A number of horsemen bound for São Paulo come riding by, and one of them, leaving his companions, quickly goes to the aid of the tottering blacks. Taking a pair of shafts upon his sturdy shoulders, he carries the litter to dry land. And Domitila de Castro, whose grandmother was Inês de Castro, rewards the young gentleman's gallant gesture with a gracious smile. The young gentleman in question was Dom Pedro, who within a few days was to become Pedro I, emperor of Brazil.

Of mixed Portuguese, Spanish, and English descent, with slight traces of Indian blood, Domitila had a pale white complexion that was set off by warm, dreamy, expressive eyes with glints of green in them; but her energetic character and her frank sensuality were evidenced not so much in her eyes as in her long pointed nose and in the capricious lines at the corners of her mouth, such a mouth as Leonardo might have painted. Tall, with a large head that looked as if it might have been carved out of marble, a shapely body, a lovely throat, a healthy rose-tinted skin, and an elegant carriage, Domitila with her smile and her soft drawling voice made the deepest impression upon the prince of any woman he had ever met in his life. She was to be his fatal love, his besetting sin that was to cause him to betray his marriage vows, resulting in a scandal that was to rock his throne.

Domitila was an ardent and vigorous young woman of twenty-four who had been the victim of an unhappy marriage that had ended in tragedy. Near her home in São Paulo, in the month of May, 1812, the imposing dragoon corps constituting the cavalry regiment of Vila Rica had been quartered. According to the Swedish observer Gustave Beyer, it was one of the most brilliant military detachments in all the world, being composed of men picked from among the leading families and clad in showy uniforms, with the finest of equipment. Felício Pinto Coelho de Mendonça, a lieutenant of the regiment and knight of the royal household, was not slow in making the acquaintance of the girl of fourteen; and it was not long before they were married, for the Castro family had their eyes on the distinguished career that awaited an officer of this select corps. Three years later a daughter was born to them, the following year a son.

One morning in March, 1819—she was in the third month of a fresh pregnancy—her husband, maddened with jealousy, stabbed her in the thigh and abdomen, leaving her bathed in her blood. The reasons for this brutal attack were never made clear, but it was rumored afterward that Domitila had accepted the attentions of Francisco de Lorena, a swaggering nobleman and officer of the headquarters staff assigned to São Paulo. Such at any rate were the accusations made by the husband in court when he sought the custody of the children.

Having been taken back into her parents' home, Domitila in August, 1819, saw her third child baptized; and three years later she crossed the prince regent's path at the very moment when he was making a deathless name for himself on the fields of Ypiranga. Inasmuch as she was a sister of Francisco de Castro Canto e Melo, his adjutant-at-arms, it was not difficult for Dom Pedro to arrange to see her during the remainder of his stay in São Paulo, and on September 9th he went back to Rio de Janeiro inflamed with love.

He was returning to consolidate the work that he had begun, to prepare to defend the country and inaugurate an American dynasty of which he was to be the founder. On his way back he rode so hard that he left his breathless escort far behind in his mad gallop, and the speediest of his companions did not reach the capital until eight hours after the prince. In the latter's ears Thomaz de Aquino's verses, which had been declaimed the evening before, were still ringing:

> Greater some day Brazil than Rome,
> With Peter its first emperor.

The twenty-three-year-old empire-builder was drunk with emotion as the streets of São Paulo echoed to the song:

> Saracura, sabiá,
> Bem-te-ví and beija-flor,*
> Let all sing, let all shout:
> Long life to our emperor!

But in Rio, neither the delirium that accompanied his acclamation and coronation nor the weight of new and absorbing cares could cause him to forget the young woman he had met in the other city. A few weeks later he persuaded the Castro family to move to the capital. He was ready to defy society, the austerity of the court, even his own consort.

On October 12th, the prince would be twenty-four years old, and this was the day chosen for his acclamation as emperor. For in addition to its Portuguese connotations, the title of king appeared too paltry a one for a country as vast as China, as big as all of Europe, and a good deal larger than the United States of North America.

Despite the heavy rain that fell, a large multitude, including six thousand soldiers, gathered in the Campo de Sant'Ana to witness the ceremony. As Dom Pedro appeared upon the tapestry-covered balcony, standing between the empress and José Clemente, president of the city council, there was an outburst of applause and *vivas,* the enthusiasm of the people reaching a high pitch as the national banner was unfurled with the imperial arms.

* These are the names of tropical birds. The saracura is a bird of a Rallidae family that inhabits swamps, lakes, and rivers. The sabiá, rendered famous in a poem by Gonçalves Dias and said to be "the only bird that sings in the rain," belongs to the Turdidae family. Bem-te-ví is the name applied to various species of Tyrannidae. The beija-flor is the hummingbird.

The crowd could scarcely hear the address delivered by José Clemente or that of Dom Pedro in which the prince declared that he accepted the title of emperor, being convinced that this was the will of all the provinces. A brilliant procession was then formed which passed between the rows of troops, beneath arches of triumph, to the imperial chapel where a solemn "Te Deum" was sung. The way was cleared by soldiers from the three branches of the service with the artillery in front, and by the procurator of the city council, carrying the gold-green standard. Then came a large gilded canopy beneath which the emperor walked with bared head; he was clad in high top boots and jingling spurs, and the stars of various military orders gleamed upon his bosom. He was followed by his ministers, the members of his court, the provincial procurators, and a huge throng of the common people.

In the throne room, shortly afterward, Dom Pedro like a radiant Caesar was to extend his hand to be kissed for the first time as a sovereign. He must have remembered that it was in this same room some years previously that he had given those fillips on the chin to the young lords in the course of a similar ceremony.

His acclamation was to be followed by his consecration and coronation. Having been anointed with the liturgical oils, he must now receive the imperial crown from the hands of the clergy. Not since the time of the great Sebastian, two and a half centuries before, had a king been crowned in Portugal with a ceremonial inspired by the legend centering about that monarch. Sebastian, so tradition had it, who had been routed by the Moors in Africa, was one day to return by a miracle of heaven, grasping the diadem with which—and with it alone—his successors were to be invested. The spectacle, therefore, was one that was new not only to America, but to many generations of Portuguese as well.

For days before, the town criers had gone through the streets loudly announcing the ceremony which was to take place on December 1st. Young lads walked ahead of them, setting off rockets to arouse the inhabitants, who came crowding to the windows. The parade, growing noisier every minute, was headed by mounted police followed by a band of music, and in the rear marched the bailiffs, the members of the city council, and other Rio notables, all in gala attire and accompanied by pages and other servants in costly liveries. The fine horses caparisoned in silver lent a still more imposing aspect to the scene as more and more persons, out of curiosity or with nothing better to do, joined the throng. Then the procession would halt, the rockets would cease, the drums would fall silent, and one of the bailiffs would step forward to read in a solemn tone of voice a document proclaiming what everyone already knew.[1]

Dom Pedro's youthful admiration for Napoleon, a source of scandal to those loyal Portuguese who had fled Lisbon to escape the haughty tyrant, led him to pattern his own coronation after that of the Corsican. In the doorway to the church, wearing gorgeous rose-hued vestments, the entire chapter of the cathedral stood waiting to cleanse the dust of this world from those who entered, by sprinkling them with holy water. Royal guardsmen marched alongside the cortege as it slowly got under way beneath the marveling gaze of the populace that lined the streets. Court functionaries and provincial procurators bore silver platters containing the royal insignia, the crown, the scepter, and the mantle, while the staff and sword were carried in the hands of the highest dignitaries.

Special places in the nave of the church and beside the great altar had been reserved for members of the upper hierarchy. Next to the throne and facing the diplomatic corps, which appeared in full dress, sat the empress, and around her were the other court ladies, all of them in white, with long gold-embroidered green velvet mantles and great clusters of white plumes upon their green and yellow turbans—green and yellow being the national colors. A green mantle lined with yellow, star-spangled and embroidered in gold—chief symbol of majesty—preserved the body of the emperor, which by this time had been anointed with the oils of David, from earthly profanation. From his throat down to the middle of his chest fell a kind of pallium woven of the feathers of the mountain cock, an extremely rare bird found in certain regions of the Amazon. Dom Pedro then mounted the throne beneath a purple velvet canopy, "against the blood-warm hue of which," says the chronicler, "the gold of galloons and fringes was joyously and gloriously reflected." [2]

Before the Mass was sung by a greatly enlarged choir, the emperor, in accordance with ancient custom, cleft the air with his sword by way of symbolizing his mission as "Perpetual Defender." In conclusion the bishop placed upon his head the imperial crown—six pounds of solid gold and diamonds—girded on his sword for him, and handed him the royal scepter. The people who crowded the neighboring streets, upon hearing that the ceremony was over, burst forth in acclamations, accompanied by the pealing of bells, fanfares, the bursting of rockets, the crack of musketry, and the thunder of cannon on land and sea. [3]

The new regime represented the Napoleonic concept applied to the Brazilian Revolution. If the kingdom stood for heredity, tradition, and divine right, the empire signified revolutionary conquest and popular acclamation. A paradoxical revolution from above, of the kind that Turgot had conceived as a means of saving Louis XVI from the tragic cataclysm of 1789, it had come to a land that had not as yet gone through the sociopolitical stages preparatory to an era of constitutional government such as that upon which the older peoples of Europe were now entering. With a heterogeneous and widely dispersed population, led by an educated and romantic-minded minority, the nation for the balance of the century was to oscillate between monarchy and democracy, liberty and authority, centralization and federation, in an effort to overcome those deficiencies that had their origin in the abrupt transition that had been effected from the status of colony to popular sovereignty. Its institutions now were being transformed not by evolution but by revolution.

In the chancelleries of Europe legitimacy was the great watchword of the day, the banner which the Holy Alliance had unfurled over the red-hot ashes of the French Revolution, but here in America it was none other than the son-in-law of His Apostolic Majesty, the emperor of Austria, who was disdainfully to give up "the divine principle" in exchange for a clamorous consecration at the hands of the masses. The guardians of worm-eaten tradition muttered against the "sacrilege"; and if their ire did not find any stronger expression, it was for the reason that the empress "by acclamation of the peoples" happened to be an Austrian archduchess, while the more clear seeing among them realized that in a continent of republics it would be still worse to permit this imitation monarchy (for in their eyes it was nothing more than that) to be extinguished. The leader of the Holy Alliance could hardly have foreseen that some seventy years later, when the Brazilian Empire had been overthrown by a military coup, the President of Colombia was mournfully to exclaim: "They have destroyed the only real republic in the Americas."

Notwithstanding the diligence of the young nation's diplomats, the courts of Europe for a period of two years withheld their recognition. The aged John VI, having been restored to absolute sovereignty by a counterrevolution in 1823, believed it still possible to reestablish the unity of the monarchy, now that

the liberal constitution had been annulled along with the brutal
and impolitic decrees of the Cortes which had been the immediate
cause of independence. With this object in view, he entrusted the
count of Rio Maior with the mission of conciliator and dispatched
him to Rio de Janeiro, but the count was not even allowed to
land. Let him return to Portugal unless, as a preliminary, he
was prepared to recognize the independence of the former colony
—such was the word sent him by Dom Pedro.

That same year, however, Pedro received a secret emissary
from John, Dom Carlos Matias Pereira, and to him the emperor
explained in minute detail the conditions that prevailed in the
country in order to show him how impossible it was to arrive at
any understanding that did not involve, *in limine,* a recognition
of independence; otherwise the vociferous opposition in the
assembly would have fresh arguments to use in inveighing against
monarchical institutions. John was very understanding and strove
to conduct himself with the greatest prudence; for he too did not
wish to offend his own subjects, who in the present instance were
more realistic than their king. Ten years later, in the course of
a speech in the Chamber of Peers, the duke of Palmela was to
bear witness to this sentiment on the part of the Portuguese. The
king, he related, had not been opposed to recognition; "the greatest difficulty had lain in placating public opinion in Portugal."
But that was something that was not so easy to do.

John's authority having been fully reestablished, the sending
of an expeditionary force for the subjugation of Brazil was definitely averted. One year after independence Palmela, in a private
communication, had revealed this fact to the count of Vila-Real.
Quite the contrary, John "would only send Portuguese troops
in order to aid the Crown Prince in putting down insurrection."
And in spite of threats and incriminations he categorically refused
to support the Russo-Spanish plan for a European congress, which

had been suggested as a means of regulating the affairs of America in accordance with the interests of legitimacy.

In August, 1825, the treaty of recognition was at last signed in Rio de Janeiro, with the English ambassador, Sir Charles Stuart, serving as mediator. In accordance with this treaty, Brazil undertook to pay £2,000,000 and John VI was to receive the honorary title of emperor of Brazil. Here was something new in the history of civilization: a people's struggle for independence that ended in the crowning of the sovereign of the mother country with the insignia of the territory he had just lost! But John was looking farther ahead than that. It was not merely out of vanity but rather from shrewd political foresight that he made a point of assuming the title against the will of all concerned, even Canning, who referred to his pretentions as "barren" ones. What His Most Faithful Majesty really desired, he who had elevated Brazil to the rank of nation and had bestowed upon it all the regalia of sovereignty, was that Dom Pedro after him should be not only emperor of Brazil, but king of Portugal as well, which was exactly what happened.

The monarchical solution had preserved the unity of Brazil by averting a prolonged crisis such as that which afflicted the other Latin American peoples, whose political apprenticeship went forward amid partisan convulsions and the clash of interests, resulting in separation and disunity. Meanwhile, the task of consolidating monarchical-liberal institutions in a land as ill prepared to receive and make use of them as was Brazil, was a Herculean one. Applying his innate liberalism at times with autocratic methods, Pedro was able to avert crises, impose discipline, calm passions, and give the nation a constitution that was to be the basic law of the land for sixty-five years.

As soon as he had been acclaimed emperor, the political fac-

tions began a campaign of agitation and engaged in a struggle
to win his favor, being eager to influence him and control his
policies. He was not the man, however, to submit to dictation,
but repelled all such attempts whether they came from parties,
social classes, or influential ministers. Without swerving either
to the right or to the left, he preserved the principle of authority,
inspired respect for institutions and strengthened them to such an
extent that, when he abdicated and returned to Europe in 1831,
the crown was able to hold out during nine years of a true republican interregnum, under regents who guided the country
until Pedro II attained his majority.

The struggle for positions of influence at court began in the
conclaves of those secret societies that played a preponderant role
in the political life of the country at this period. Two rival
branches of Masonry were struggling energetically to get the
upper hand with the prince, but he evaded their traps by crushing
both of them. Immediately afterward, the struggle between the
Constituent Assembly and the emperor degenerated into demagogic excesses which at one time threatened to do away with
the crown's prerogatives. Pedro then had the assembly chamber
cleared with bayonets and deported the principal leaders, after
which he himself granted a constitution that Chateaubriand did
not hesitate to condemn for its "exaggerated democratic character."

Masonry, which had reached a high state of development in
Portugal under the ministry of the marquis of Pombal, had
sprung up in Brazil at the end of the colonial era. Arruda Câmara,
a former Carmelite friar and a physician of the faculty of medicine
of Montpellier, had founded the first lodge in 1794, on the border-
line of the provinces of Pernambuco and Paraíba under the name
of the Areopagus of Itambé. In 1801, a mysterious "Chevalier

Laurent" was to preside over the installation in Rio de Janeiro of the "Union" lodge, a secret organization with a ritual and with sociopolitical objectives, affiliated to the Orient of the Ile-de-France. Two years later, the Lusitanian Grand Orient supervised the organization of regular lodges in Rio, thereby providing a common center for all the Masons in the capital. It also initiated new members and conferred degrees up to that of Grand Master, which was as far as its authorization went.[4]

These, so to speak, were the first "official" branches of the order in Brazil, but secret organizations more or less modeled after the Masons had existed for many years. A French captain by the name of Landolphe, who had been imprisoned along the Brazilian coast in the year 1800 and who had been turned over to the Count of Rezende, the viceroy, states in his *Memoirs* that he was especially well treated for the reason that he was a Freemason. Having been taken by the viceroy's son to a Masonic meeting, he was filled with astonishment at "seeing in that place, among the chief military leaders and administrators of the colony, some of the highest dignitaries of the Church." In May, 1822, accompanying the movement for separation, there was established a high Masonic body known as the Grand Orient of Brazil, with three metropolitan lodges of liberal, semirepublican tendencies. Two opposing groups then sprang up within these societies: an ultraliberal one led by Gonçalves Ledo; and a conservative faction headed by José Bonifácio de Andrada e Silva, the most distinguished Brazilian of his time and Dom Pedro's minister and chief adviser, a man of great culture, energy, and character.

Although he had been elected Grand Master of the Orient, José Bonifácio found that this society was in reality under the control of Ledo, who had been elected Senior Warden, and his group; and so, five days later, with the support of Dom Pedro he founded a new and independent one entitled the "Apostolate of the Noble Order of the Knights of the Holy Cross," taking with him the conservative and monarchical wing of Masonry. Under the name of Romulus and with the title of Archon-King, Dom Pedro on June 22nd assumed the direction of this "Apostolate," which was the means that José Bonifácio counted upon for crushing his enemies of the Grand Orient. The latter, in turn, were also ambitious to control the prince and gain for themselves the favor which the aged minister enjoyed at court, and they accordingly sought to attract the monarch to their secret meeting places by every means in their power.

Being aware of the strength and influence that masonry exerted and desiring to dominate the revolution that it sponsored with the purpose of eventually giving it a monarchical orientation, Dom Pedro permitted himself to become involved in the plot that had been carefully worked out by the Grand Orient. Having been admitted to the session of July 13, 1822, he was received in the "Reflection Chamber" and regularly initiated with all the customary tests. He took for himself the heroic name of Guatimozin, and as a special privilege was accorded a seat in the Orient. Three days later, the "Apprentice" Guatimozin was elevated to the degree of "Master" on the motion of Gonçalves Ledo; and immediately afterward, he was invested with all the Masonic degrees and elected Grand Master to take the place of José Bonifácio. Such was the clever plan by which the Senior Warden hoped to deprive the minister of his prestige while flattering the prince's vanity and winning the royal favor.

On the very night of his return from São Paulo, one week after he had uttered the historic "Cry of Ypiranga," Dom Pedro visited the Masonic Lodge in order to be inaugurated as Grand Master. Conducted by Ledo to the altar, he took the oath and was duly proclaimed, recognized, and applauded as he received the Grand Gavel and entered upon the duties of his office. José Bonifácio was absent that night, and without his being given a chance to be heard he was now demoted by Ledo from Grand Master to Assistant Grand Master, an especially created and meaningless post. Ledo's speech upon this occasion, addressed to Dom Pedro, was a veritable manifesto on the part of the opposition, aimed at the influential minister: "Beware, O worthy Grand Master, of choleric men and those ridden by their passions. However learned they may be, they never attain to sound judgment but are inclined always to wrongdoing. Do not give yourself over to the wicked ones, but put your trust in your own loyal Masons. . . ."

The question of the so called "preliminary oath" then came up. Before being acclaimed emperor, Dom Pedro must swear to uphold the constitution to be adopted by the Constituent Assembly. The monarch was far from being opposed to this, and indeed, in the Grand Orient where the idea originated, he declared that "if it was for the good of Brazil and the tranquillity of the people, he was willing to take two or three oaths, if necessary." The point at issue, however—though the prince did not perceive it—was an essential one. Having taken this "preliminary oath," he would be hopelessly handcuffed to the assembly and forced to accept its decisions whatever they might be. Just as had happened in Portugal, once the assembly had obtained a monopoly of the legislative authority it would be able to override the sovereign's will.

José Bonifácio, with his experience and political adroitness, did not fail to see what the purpose of this maneuver was; and being bound to safeguard the monarch's rights, he conceived the idea of involving the people themselves in the act of acclamation so that the assembly when it met would find Dom Pedro already invested with power without its intervention: emperor by direct will of the people. Pedro, on the other hand, who at first sight did not get the full meaning of it all, not only agreed to the preliminary oath, but went so far as to entrust to Ledo and his lieutenants, José Clemente and Nóbrega, three sheets of blank paper bearing his signature. This triumph for the Grand Orient, which felt that it now had the young prince in its power, was to lead to its own downfall. Upon coming to his senses, thanks chiefly to José Bonifácio, Pedro sent for Ledo and demanded that the documents be returned to him, or otherwise the three who held them would be imprisoned in the harbor fortress. And the threat was repeated to José Clemente, president of the city council of Rio de Janeiro, in case he insisted upon enforcing the oath. For his own part, José Bonifácio at once mobilized his "apostles," and the streets were soon filled with popular groups demanding the deportation of the principal officers of the Grand Orient. The assembly next day withdrew the clause referring to the preliminary oath.

At the first signs of insubordination on the part of the Grand Orient, Dom Pedro in a communication of only five lines dissolved that body until further notice and had its leaders arrested, taken to the fortresses, and deported for France on board the brig *La Cécile*. The Senior Warden Ledo went into hiding; and then one night, with his face, breast, and arms painted black, dressed like a woman, and with a basket on his head, he made his way to Niterói, where he managed to embark for Buenos Aires thanks to the protection afforded him by the Swedish consul. Within forty-eight hours Dom Pedro had completely destroyed the organization that had caused court and ministers to tremble and had undertaken to dictate his own imperial acts.

José Bonifácio had won a victory but he hardly was in a position to foresee the nearing blow that Dom Pedro was to deal him. Poet, philosopher, man of law, mineralogist with a reputation throughout all Europe, and former counselor to John VI, he had as his most characteristic trait a violent disposition and an overweening consciousness of his own worth. An exalted patriot, an ardent and combative politician, he has been well described by a French diplomat as *"une tête volcanique avec des cheveux blancs."* Dom Pedro's chief minister since the eve of independence, he had advised him wisely and intelligently and rightly deserved the appellation of "Patriarch of Independence." If Dom Pedro was the arm, José Bonifácio was the brains of the movement.

How highly the monarch valued him is indicated by an anecdote. The French consul was riding past the door of the minister's house one day just as Dom Pedro was entering it, and overheard the following bit of dialogue in the street:

"Is that the prince regent?"

"Yes, that is the prince, José Bonifácio's aide-de-camp."

The sternness with which the minister prosecuted his enemies, especially those of the Grand Orient, won for him the hatred and resentment of all classes. In the provinces he had the opponents of the government tracked down, their movements spied upon, and their subversive plottings crushed with fire and sword. Through the Austrian ambassador in Rio de Janeiro he found a contact with Metternich, supreme pontiff of the Holy Alliance, who encouraged and warmly applauded his uncompromising attitude in defense of the imperial authority. Being informed as to all this and temperamentally opposed to persecution and the harboring of grudges, Pedro decided to put an end to the situation by stopping the prosecution then under way in São Paulo, the object of which was to bring to justice those responsible for the disorders in the month of August; José Bonifácio, who was in charge of the matter, was thereby forced to resign along with his brother, Martim Francisco, who held the portfolio of finance.

This news burst like a bombshell in Vienna. De Gentz, Metternich's principal aide, exclaimed that the prince had "given fresh proof of his weakness of character and a weak-mindedness that bordered on dementia." In his proclamation addressed to the Brazilians, Dom Pedro had employed the words "My constitutional rights," and this greatly exasperated the distinguished publicist. "How does that sound in the mouth of a prince, I ask you! How we have fallen!"

Dom Pedro at that moment had been confined to his bed for more than two weeks. On June 30th (1823), a serious accident had resulted in two broken ribs, a dislocated collarbone, and a grave injury to his hip. Yet he managed to climb the stairs of São Cristovão supported only by a cane; and on the following day, although he was exhausted from bleeding—they had applied a total of nineteen leeches in the region of the thigh—he gave an audience of one hour to the French ambassador, who wrote home to his government that he was astonished at the monarch's "endurance and *sang-froid*." [5]

On July 15th the treasurer of the imperial household received a letter from some unknown person; it was written in German and was to be delivered at once into the emperor's own hand or otherwise his life would be in imminent danger. Translated by the empress, the letter revealed the fact that the "Apostles," taking advantage of their sovereign's absence, had formed a conspiracy against his life and with this object in view were to hold a meeting that same night. Dom Pedro thereupon rose from bed just as he was, still swathed in bandages, and muffling himself in a cape he set out at once for the artillery barracks in São Cristovão. Around eight that night he left there accompanied by a group of officers and soldiers who were in his confidence.

They were mounted on unshod horses, all of them, and they made straight for the rua da Guarda-Velha, where the "Apostolate" was located. When the door was opened after the conventional knocks were given, Dom Pedro thrust aside the doorkeeper, who had recognized him and attempted to bar his way; he did the same to a second one and then burst into the meeting room. In accordance with their custom upon the arrival of any member of their order, the Apostles arose and raised their daggers in the air. Restraining his companions who, ignorant of this ritual, had drawn their swords to defend him, Dom Pedro put them out into the anteroom and proceeded to enter alone. Making his way among those upraised daggers, he strode resolutely forward to the throne of the Archon-King where, vastly astonished at the emperor's arrival, a third brother of José Bonifácio, Antônio Carlos, leader of the Constituent Assembly, was presiding. When the latter, in the act of offering his seat, attempted to pick up the minutes of the meeting where the conspirators' plans were set forth, Pedro stopped him, took possession of the documents himself, and in the strongest of language ordered the conspirators to leave the room. Trembling with fright, they made their escape between the rows of soldiers drawn up outside.[6]

Highly wrought up over what had occurred and nursing a deep resentment, José Bonifácio and his brothers, immediately following the break with Dom Pedro, joined the ranks of the oppositionists in the Constituent Assembly, bringing with them the weight of their prestige, their gift of eloquence, and fund of energy. In the pages of *Tamoyo,* a militant Jacobin organ, they began a violent campaign against the emperor, seeking to alienate his enormous popular following. The leading orator of the assembly and its true leader from the beginning, Antônio Carlos found full scope for his talents and a vent for his pride in the formidable attacks he now launched against the young ruler. Inasmuch as Pedro was Portuguese by birth, the keynote of the campaign was one of suspicion and discrimination against those who were Brazilian by adoption; by arousing the suspicion of an intended union with Portugal, the oppositionists sought to gain the sympathy of the people and undermine their respect for the crown.

From the opening sessions the mutual lack of understanding between the assembly and the emperor was all too apparent. The latter's right to veto the constitution that was voted in case he did not deem it "worthy of himself and of the nation" was the touchstone of all discussions. Each side, for reasons of self-preservation, sought to limit, or at any rate offset, those prerogatives of the other side that were inimical to its own. The assembly, which was a legislative as well as a constituent body, resolved by a majority of four votes that its decrees should be promulgated without need of an imperial sanction; the role of the sovereign was to be limited to carrying them out. Carneiro de Campos, José Bonifácio's successor in the council of ministers, was of a calm and conciliatory temperament, and he advised Dom Pedro to appease the deputies, seeing that this was merely a temporary measure, until the constitution, which contained no such provision, should be proclaimed; the assembly's resolution, therefore, did not greatly matter.

The timidity and moderation of the new ministers encouraged the assembly to resist the threats and intimations of the crown. The language of *Tamoyo* and other opposition newspapers increased in violence. First the ministers and then the emperor himself were attacked in most unbridled fashion, and some even went so far as an open incitation to revolution: "A government that goes counter to the will of the nation must be overthrown at once. . . . It is dangerous to drive the people to despair and force them to demand by violence that which they as yet seek only by constitutional means." Then came allusions to the execution of Charles I, Louis XVI, the expulsion of the Stuarts from the English throne, and to those sovereigns who had ended their lives upon the scaffold or in exile.

It was a comparatively minor incident that provoked the final explosion. Two Portuguese officers who had been violently attacked by *Tamoyo* had chastised with their canes the supposed author of the articles, the apothecary Daví Pamplona. The victim of the assault having been called in, the assembly with passions highly inflamed proceeded to set itself up as a tribunal and undertook to banish the accused with the object of arousing hatred against the Portuguese. It was found afterward that Pamplona was as much a Portuguese as were his assailants, but he nevertheless was held up as an "innocent Brazilian who had been insulted and beaten, the defenseless victim of Lusitanian arrogance." This uncalled-for meddling by the assembly in what was strictly a matter for the police and the judiciary was instigated by Antônio Carlos, who by way of arousing the enthusiasm of the packed galleries, shouted: "In view of this nefarious assault, I instinctively cry, Vengeance!" His brother, Martim Francisco, went further still. Expressing astonishment that the assailants were still alive, he cried: "Ah! the infamous ones! To think that they go on living and that we must put up with such wild beasts in our midst!"

The assembly having been declared in permanent session in order that it might demand of the government an explanation of certain precautionary measures of a military nature that had been taken, Dom Pedro made up his mind to dissolve it. He had yielded too much already, had temporized too long, had acquiesced in all its excesses. But now it was no longer a mere lack of discipline with which he had to deal; the assembly was within a step of revolution. Without asking his ministers' advice, he showed them on the morning of November 11th the decree of dissolution he had already drawn up for them to countersign. Two of them refused, and he dismissed them on the spot. Detachments of artillery and cavalry accompanied the general who bore the order to the assembly. Between the ranks of soldiers the deputies left the hall; there was very little turbulence now, for the principal leaders of the opposition had already been arrested and deported, among them José Bonifácio and his brothers, who were to spend nearly seven years in exile.

A council of state, composed of eminent citizens, now began the work of preparing the constitution under the emperor's personal direction. In a certain sense it was more liberal than the one proposed by the assembly—Dom Pedro had promised that —and at the same time this Magna Charta was better suited to the political conditions that prevailed in the country. Granting the sovereign the powers of a moderator, it assured him that minimum of centralization that was indispensable to the preservation of national unity, which had by no means been firmly established as yet. Led by a Carmelite monk, Friar Caneca, a brave and ardent patriot, the province of Pernambuco now rose in defense of the Constituent Assembly, but Pedro managed to assemble a fairly impressive naval force and put down the rebellion. Unrelenting on this occasion, he did nothing to prevent the monk from going to the scaffold. For he could withhold mercy at times, bestow it at other times.

"When the Fatherland is suffering," the rebel had shouted, "the eyes of the patriot are blind to everything else: to the wails of little children, the tears of the wife, and the parent's lament. Patriotism is the only language he knows."

Dom Pedro took a delight in bestowing liberty, but let them not attempt to deprive him of it. He would defend his prerogatives with tooth and nail, displaying all the vigor of a soldier and the aggressiveness of a despot. He would strike down liberals to show himself more liberal than they, and remorselessly trample them under foot as if to rid himself of competitors even in the realm of the ideal.

CHAPTER EIGHT

DOM PEDRO'S DOUBLE LIFE

Yielding with good grace to the young sovereign's ardent entreaties, Domitila hastened to exchange her provincial obscurity for the brilliant social life of the court at Rio de Janeiro. She was accompanied by her parents, her two brothers who were cavalry lieutenants, and a married sister. The first year went by tranquilly enough, the emperor taking pains to avoid any appearance of scandal in his relations with the beautiful Paulista. The divorce suit that she had brought and that had been dragging along in a maze of legal technicalities was now speeded up, resulting in a judgment favoring the plaintiff, with Lieutenant Felício giving up all claims to the children.

Day by day Dom Pedro became more and more enamored of Domitila's charms, and it was said that this passion was due to a spell cast upon him by a black man's magic potion which had enslaved the emperor forever to that pair of deep-glowing eyes. Hearing that the favorite's former husband, who at this time was administrator of the plantation of Periperí, had once more been making insulting remarks about her, Pedro, despite the fact that it was a stormy night, covered the distance of a little more than forty miles on horseback, roundly slapped the disgruntled lieutenant's face, and obliged him to sign a paper swear-

ing that he would never again molest his former wife, under pain
of another thrashing.

As his love for his mistress increased, the monarch showered
more and more favors and posts of honor upon her family.
Shocked by the affair, the prudish court was already beginning
to talk, and these rumors soon spread to the general public, always
curious and eager where scandals of this sort are concerned. In
September, 1824, there occurred the incident of the "Little
Theater of São Pedro," and tongues began wagging all over town.
This theater, supported by amateurs, was one of the select meeting
places of Rio de Janeiro. Probably out of a desire to meet the
fashionable nobility, Domitila put in an appearance there one
night. Having been refused entrance on the ground that she did
not have a special invitation, there was nothing for her to do
but leave, in deep humiliation; but Dom Pedro, when he heard
of the matter, at once had the theater closed, the company dissolved, and ordered the premises vacated without delay.

Wrapped up in her mineralogy and the theories of Newton
and Laplace, the empress, at least down to the end of the year
1825, gave no sign of suspecting the liaison; Dom Pedro and
Domitila in turn sought to avoid in her presence any look, word,
or gesture that might compromise them. The Austrian minister
Mareschal, who had accompanied Leopoldina to look after her,
just as Count Mercy did Marie Antoinette, wrote home to
Vienna: "Notwithstanding the fact that he has a favorite mistress,
he has never ceased for an instant to show himself a good husband,
and takes advantage of every opportunity to praise the virtues
of his consort."

One day, at the very moment when he was writing to
Domitila, Pedro suddenly became aware that Leopoldina had
entered the room. He hastily hid the letter until his wife had left
and then took it out and added a postscript: "The Empress came

near catching me in the act, but your prayers saved me." In his letters the emperor frequently sets forth the means by which they are to carry on this dissimulation: "It is better when I go out in the daytime that I should not come past for a word with you, in order that she may not suspect our—our holy love—and this, even if I have to go out of my way; and it is also best for me not to speak of you at home but rather of any other woman whatsoever, in order that she may suspect another and we may go on living in peace and enjoying this wonderful love of ours." [1]

In 1825, on the occasion of the Holy Week ceremonies in the imperial chapel, one of Dom Pedro's chamberlains inadvertently seated Domitila in the pew reserved for the ladies of the court, a number of whom, offended by the favorite's presence among them—for the gossip about her was steadily increasing—promptly retired out of spite, as a sign of protest to be witnessed by all those present. The empress, however, being innately kind and wholly unaware of the rumors associated with Domitila's name, out of a desire to make public amends for the insult, had her appointed her first lady in waiting. Thus, like Catherine de Medici, Marie d'Anjou, and so many other queens, Leopoldina was to see her rival installed in the intimacy of the royal apartments for the greater convenience of the lovers.

Domitila's presentation at court was a gala affair. All in white, with a garland of rosebuds adorning her silky, well-cared-for hair, smiling radiantly and bursting with happiness, the courtesan entered the reception room. Dom Pedro did not dare accompany her into his wife's presence but delegated to one of the court ladies, Francisca de Castelo Branco, this act of gallantry which, had he followed the dictates of his heart, he would have performed himself, but for which he lacked the courage. [2]

Inconsistent in carrying out his resolve to conceal their love in so far as possible from the eyes of his wife, the emperor on

October 12, 1825, elevated Domitila to the nobility by making her Viscountess of Santos, at the same time conferring honorary titles upon two of her brothers. Thus, with a single stroke of the pen, he at once flattered his mistress and struck out at his enemies, those haughty Andrada brothers, who were natives of the city of Santos. The exiled José Bonifácio, when he heard of it, was furious. "Who," he cried, "would ever have dreamed that a creature like Domitila would be viscountess of the homeland of the Andradas? What a crackbrained insult!" But Dom Pedro, who was in a state of foolish bliss, only smiled.

The year before, on the 23rd of May, the first fruit of this illegitimate union was born—a daughter, Isabel, presented at the baptismal font as being a child of unknown parentage, who had been left at the home of Domitila's father, Colonel João de Castro. On December 7th of the following year, Domitila gave birth to a son, Pedro de Alcântara Brasileiro, five days after the empress had borne the future Pedro II. For the next four years the two women, the lawful wife and the concubine, were to keep on conceiving and bearing young ones simultaneously, bringing into the world an abundance of princes and bastards.

It appears that it was not until the beginning of 1826, on a voyage to the province of Bahia, that Leopoldina became clearly aware of the romance that for three years past had been affording a fragrant variation in diplomatic dispatches while stimulating the intrigues of fetch-and-carry courtiers. Upon the deck of the *Pedro I*—eight maids of honor, among them Domitila, had accompanied the sovereigns, not to speak of a numerous retinue of noblemen and major-domos—the emperor, lulled by the lapping of the waves and the long hours of calm on shipboard, must have had little control over his impulses; for he imprudently called his mistress by her pet name, "Titilia," without taking care to see that no talebearers were near. And then, when the empress had retired below deck, avoiding the conversation of courtiers and ministers, he would go look for the viscountess until he found her leaning over the rail beneath the captain's awning and gazing up at the stars with a faraway look in her eyes. Suspicious at first, later convinced, Leopoldina undoubtedly must have found means of confining to her cabin of a night the maid of honor who was her rival.[3]

The province of Bahia for almost a year had borne the brunt of the struggle against the Portuguese forces of occupation. For this reason Dom Pedro wished to visit it, that he might personally decorate the heroes of the resistance, learn the needs of the province, and complete the task of uniting it to the central government. His joviality, his frank, straightforward way of speaking, and his tireless activity delighted the Bahians, who cheered him wherever he went, in the arsenals, in the streets and public squares, in the hospitals, churches, prisons, and government buildings, all of which he zealously inspected as he went about deciding what steps were to be taken, dictating decrees to his secretaries of state, pardoning deserters, creating barons.

Twelve days after his arrival the British ambassador, Sir Charles Stuart, put in an appearance. He was in a very bad humor and complained of not having been formally advised of His Majesty's embarkation. After signing the treaty of recognition on behalf of Portugal, the British diplomat had entered into negotiations with the Brazilian government regarding a treaty of friendship, commerce, and navigation, and a covenant for the abolition of the slave trade. In a letter to his minister Vilela Barbosa, Dom Pedro himself has described this meeting with Stuart.

"I have come to Bahia," the Englishman began, "to speak to Your Majesty regarding certain matters now pending between our two countries." There was a trace of arrogance in his manner.

"Very well," Dom Pedro interrupted him, "so far as speaking to me goes, Your Excellency has already done that; and so far as official business is concerned, it is impossible for me to discuss it, since I do not have my council of state here."

Far from being disconcerted by this ill natured reply, the diplomat grew more impertinent. He began complaining about the Brazilian ministers and evinced displeasure at the fact that Dom Pedro had not waited for him, concluding with the hint that he would like to go back to London. With this, the emperor lost control of himself and roared at the audacious Britisher:

"You may go wherever you wish, sir. It makes no difference to me one way or the other. As to my not having waited for you, I would have you know that I would not have waited for the king of England, much less for you. Upon leaving, I had the ship's gun fired for the precise purpose of letting you know that I was going and did not care to wait. And do not come around to me again with any revelations as to how Bolívar with twelve thousand men is marching on our frontiers. I am not afraid of the king of France, nor the king of England, nor anyone else. I am a man who knows how to die sword in hand. As for you, sir, if you have any business to transact with me, go back to Rio and wait. I shall set sail on the 12th." [4]

With these words, the emperor turned and left him.

Upon her return from Bahia, Domitila went to live in a large mansion in the rua Nova do Imperador, directly opposite the main entrance to the Boa Vista Gardens. An architect of the imperial household, Pedro Alexandre Cavroé, had seen to remodeling it inside and out, while the murals were done by the distinguished Mulatto, Francisco Pedro do Amaral, chief painter and decorator to His Imperial Majesty. The location of the house could not have been better for the two lovers. From the great towers of the palace, spyglass in hand, Dom Pedro could see his mistress's windows, and, by means of mimicry, exchange signals and messages with her. Innumerable notes testify to the extensive use that was made of this optical communication at a distance:

Let me know who is there; I can see from here two chaises standing in front of the house. . . . You were seated at the window but did not answer my signal, although I was looking through my glass for a sight of you. . . . I was about to have supper; it was around twenty minutes of nine, and I saw that you were very prudently accompanied by a taper.[5]

On May 24, 1826, Dom Pedro awed his subjects with a bold decree officially recognizing as his daughter little Isabel, the first child he had had by the Viscountess of Santos. A change was accordingly made in the baptismal register, and in place of the notation "Of unknown parentage," the curate made an entry to show that the father of Isabel Maria de Alcântara Brasileiro was none other than the emperor himself. Dom Pedro was growing more fond each day of this child who was now completing her third year, and could not bear such a stigma on her name. The institutions of the country might be shaken to their foundations, but that infant should not go through life under the disgrace of having been a castaway!

The viscountess then gave a brilliant banquet at her home, at which, in addition to the emperor himself in full-dress uniform, thirty or forty courtiers, ministers, and councilors of state were present. A little more than a month later, Dom Pedro bestowed upon the child the title of Duchess of Goiaz, with the provision that she was to be addressed as Your Highness; and he sent out the proper notices to the military authorities regarding the formalities that were to be observed toward her.

His extreme fondness for children, whether legitimate or not, was one of the outstanding traits of his character. The Austrian minister Mareschal more than once came upon him in his shirt sleeves, playing in the palace with his children, who adored him. Writing to Vienna, Leopoldina frequently speaks of the charming manner in which her husband treated their first-born, Maria da Gloria: "He is the best of fathers; always playing with her, he carries her in his arms all the time we are out walking and is never tired of caressing her."

The slightest indisposition, the most ordinary illness would arouse his paternal apprehensions and he would become extremely attentive. If it was necessary to give them medicine, vaccinate or purge them, he himself did it zealously and skillfully. Writing to Domitila, he tells her:

Maria Isabel was vaccinated by me today. . . . There is nothing the matter with the child; she slept well, but the only thing is she had difficulty in moving her bowels; I am going to give her some Viennese Water, which ought to help her. . . . Mariquita has taken an ounce of Water and still no action; I gave her another and she vomited; and if she does not have an action within the next three hours, I shall give her some more. . . . The Duchess has a high color and there are dried sores on her skin.

Far from being well educated himself, Pedro was seriously concerned with his children's studies. To Maria da Gloria he wrote: "I was glad to receive your letter; it is better written than the others, but if in place of spending the whole morning in bed, you would devote yourself to study, then there would not be any mistakes at all." Laboring over his shaky syntax, he concludes, severely: "When I see you, I shall ask for an accounting, from you and from your teacher." For the crown prince, the future Pedro II of Brazil, who was to be known as the "philosopher king," he was to procure the best of teachers and the wisest of counsellors; and writing to his son from Europe, after his abdication, he constantly urges the strictest application to studies: "Yes, my beloved son, this is very necessary in order that you may assure the well-being of Brazil."

With an unruly youth behind him, he who had grown up in the stables was to give the royal governesses and tutors such instructions as the following to the Countess of Itapagipe: "Above all I ask of you that you see to it that my children are well behaved toward everyone, that their manners are refined and that when they converse, they choose their words carefully and pronounce them clearly. I also beg you not to permit in their presence any conversation that may be harmful to their morals, for this is something that should never happen among persons of good breeding." Upon this point the monarch, who had spent his childhood and a good part of his adolescence among boys from the street and other rowdies, was insistent: "Be careful," he instructed Dona Marianna, "to preserve the respect that is due my children, and by no manner of means should you permit strangers or those who are ill educated or whose conduct is not all it should be to have any dealings or conversation with them. . . . I trust you to exercise the utmost care in this regard and to guide them in the path of virtue by lessons and good examples."

It was Dom Pedro's custom to observe his birthday by granting titles, decorations, and rewards, promoting dignitaries and other public officials, and freeing prisoners who had been condemned to the galleys. On October 12, 1826, the entire country as usual eagerly perused the list of imperial favors as published in the *Diário Fluminense*. The public could not have been more surprised. It found that the emperor by his decrees had made Domitila Marchioness of Santos while her father became the

Viscount de Castro. All her brothers were elevated to gentlemanly rank, one of them being made a colonel; two of her relatives were appointed to the royal wardrobe, and a brother-in-law was created Baron of Sorocaba! Never had there been seen such a deluge of honors upon a single family. The influence of the favorite now reached its apex. The toadies hovered about her more and more, while those that were passed over went to swell the chorus of whisperers in the clubs of the opposition even as patriots were lamenting the demoralization of the crown and Leopoldina was shedding heartfelt tears. As for Dom Pedro, he merely shrugged his shoulders.

His submission to his mistress was absolute. He was hopelessly in love with her and was jealous of her very shadow. He would frequently indulge in wild ravings and outbursts of anger, after which he would meekly beg her pardon as he protested his passion for her, yielded to her every whim, and invented small afflictions to arouse her sympathy. Possessed of a strong character and a great deal of personality, Domitila during those seven years that she spent as the emperor's concubine was to conduct herself in a natural manner without any major excesses or unseemly behavior. She put on the airs of a great lady and succeeded in making herself respected by all, including Dom Pedro—especially Dom Pedro. She was never cowed by the monarch's fits of irritation but would face him proudly and repel him haughtily. Aware that he had gone too far, Pedro would humble himself: "Tonight I shall have the pleasure (for me a very great one) of being with you and I hope to be a polished gentleman so that you will not have to call me a boor."

Here was an emperor who had an entire nation at his feet, who had overturned idols, crushed conspiracies, defied potentates, and commanded armies; but he was not to dominate this headstrong young woman whom he had brought up from the depths of the provinces. In the copious correspondence that passed between him and his mistress, their romance is vividly reflected as in a mirror. We behold him always amorous and impetuous, a "loyal, constant, eager, and grateful lover." She on the other hand is discreet and respectable, generally amiable though sometimes complaining, sometimes cold, rarely exuberant. When she does let herself go a bit, Dom Pedro is delighted: "I thank you very much for the kiss and the embrace that you sent me in your note; I appreciate it all the more since it is not by way of reward but comes of your own free will."

There were jealous scenes now and then. "I do not care to take second place to anyone, not even to God, if that were possible," he wrote on one occasion. In the theater he watched the glances which she bestowed on others: "I may tell you that your habit of looking up at the ceiling when I catch you gazing at others is not very clever." And another time: "How can you expect me not to have doubts when they are born of love?" Becoming violent on meeting a young officer who was leaving the marchioness's house at an unseemly hour, the emperor chastised the intruder with his riding whip and in return became the target for a pistol bullet which, however, lodged in a Bordone painting on the wall, the "Coronation of the Doge Mascantoni."

Domitila likewise kept a jealous watch over her lover. When she had a presentiment that her sister, the baroness of Sorocaba, was about to yield to Dom Pedro's insistencies, she became indignant and, so it would appear, even plotted against the life of her rival. The fact is that on an August night in 1828 someone discharged a blunderbuss into the Baroness's carriage, and it was only by a miracle that she escaped unharmed.

The favorite made no attempt at concealment when her feelings were hurt. One day after they had had a slight tiff, she caught sight of the emperor watching her through his spyglass, whereupon she did not hesitate to have all the windows slammed shut. Dom Pedro at once sent her an angry note: "Much obliged for shutting the windows just when I was trying to get a sight of you." And then, after venting his anger at length, he adds a gentler postscript: "Forgive me if I use strong language, but it is my heart, which belongs to you, that is speaking."

Dom Pedro's love was deep and irrepressible. "My girl," he writes, "if I am sometimes a bit rude with you, this is due to my despair at not being able to enjoy your company as much as I should like. This it is that makes me do such things. They do not come from the heart, for my heart adores you, and always feels for you something that I cannot express." But despite his good resolves, he was not able to restrain his impulsive outbursts, which Domitila found it hard to forgive. "My girl, do not hold it against me; for I love you with all my heart, and just because I do love you so much and am absolutely frank with you, a frankness that you do not return, I sometimes say things that I ought not to, and for which I beg your forgiveness." Or again: "Forgive me for having made you angry, as I could be accused of no greater fault than having offended you ever so slightly." At other times he is delicate and formal: "I shall be very happy if you will pardon any improper language on my part."

Even when Dom Pedro is aware that she is wholly to blame, if Domitila holds out, he ends by giving in to her: "I am sorry that you will not admit it so that we might beg each other's pardon." When he indicates his desire to visit her, it is never in a tone of command: "My girl, if you will give me permission, I should like to come to see you tomorrow night; in which case, will you see to having me admitted? . . . Permit me, my girl, to come tonight." One time he complains: "I cannot get you to write me saying 'You may come'; but in spite of my illness, I shall be there anyway." In the same note, however, a few lines below, he softens this statement somewhat: "Let me know if I may come, and see that the door is open."

Many writers insist upon beholding in Domitila a "Brazilian Pompadour," an adventuress who had the reins of government in her hands, giving and countermanding orders and settling affairs of state. The truth is that she was too feminine to mingle in heated partisan struggles. As a pretty woman, she was always a good deal more interested in her attire and other fineries than in political matters; although it cannot be denied that it was her interference in one or two prominent cases that made her a subject of interest to all classes of society. Loyal to her friends, she obtained for them promotions, honorary titles, appointments, and other small favors which the passionate Braganza did not begrudge her; and this was enough to excite the fury of her enemies.

She knew her power, but the curious thing is that she never abused it. She never made use of her standing at court to persecute the disaffected or to create prejudice against them or injure them in any way. As a rule, when she did intervene it was from generous motives, with the object of placating the monarch's wrath, restraining his impulsiveness, or making up for his rudeness. In her correspondence she is to be found, a number of times, appealing to Dom Pedro's clemency: "I beg you not to do anything to José and Marcolino." On one occasion the emperor replies to her: "I have just this moment given Martins a total pardon and have ordered his release."

As for Leopoldina, she never revealed her suffering in public, or in the presence of her husband, but stifled her sobs deep in her heart. To judge by her apparent imperturbability and self-respecting manner, she had even come to view with indifference not only the favorite who came and went through her apartments like one of the family, but the little duchess of Goiaz, also, who played with the emperor's legitimate children. As if rendered impatient by this display of coldness, the French ambassador Gestas wrote to his government: "The Empress's self-restraint is sometimes carried to the point of insouciance as regards the liaison of her august Consort with Madame de Santos." The Austrian minister in turn informed Vienna: "It appears to me impossible that Madame the Archduchess does not see what is going on under her very eyes."

Leopoldina, meanwhile, saw and kept silent. Not until much later were her feelings revealed through the publication of her letters to her sister and to her devoted friend Schaeffer. To the latter she wrote concerning the Duchess of Goiaz: "I could bear anything, as I have in the past, except seeing the little one treated as my children's equal; I tremble with rage when I look at her, and it is the greatest sacrifice on my part to receive her." Nor did she spare Domitila: "Here, everything is upside down; for speaking in all sincerity, infamous women like Pompadour and Maintenon, especially when they are possessed of no education whatsoever, . . ." and so forth.

Her love for Dom Pedro was something irresistible and overwhelming. When she was with him, she forgot as if by enchantment all her wrongs and humiliations, merely to enjoy for the moment the permanent object of her thoughts and of her disquieting dreams. She did not know how to contend against the favorite and never made any attempt to do so. Without any sign of reaction, she continued to be negligent of her clothes and hair and averse to cosmetics and coquetry of any kind. Her great friend Jacques Arago has drawn a sincere portrait of her: "Not to exaggerate in the least, she was dressed like a true gypsy, down to the slippers, even; no necklace, no earrings, not a ring on her fingers." It was not until October, 1826, after the concubine had been made Marchioness of Santos, that Leopoldina for the first time voiced an open protest by revealing to the Austrian minister how unhappy she was and charging him to notify the emperor, her father, of the fact.

A short while afterward, a second and more serious cause of friction arose when Viscount de Castro, the marchioness's father, died. For two whole days and nights, without leaving the bedside, Dom Pedro watched over the old colonel in his last agony. In the palace, surrounded by her children, Leopoldina bitterly endured his prolonged absence and when at last she saw her husband coming in and looking downcast over the event, she impulsively gave way to despair, threw off the passivity of four long years, and berated him rudely. She would retire to a convent until her father sent for her. Stunned by this, the emperor retorted with grave insults.

They were soon reconciled; but the empress, whose health had been seriously affected ever since the difficult time she had had in bearing young Prince Pedro, now fell into a deep melancholy. Overcome by depression, she gave up her customary walks and horseback rides, her cheeks lost their color and her enviable vigor and good health rapidly disappeared. Only the sight of her "beloved Pedro" gave her the animation to light up with a wan smile a face that was growing thinner day by day. The emperor surrounded her with every sign of tenderness and affection, sought to keep her company, strove to mitigate the growing pain she felt and to console her during those long nights when she was so sleepless and depressed. But it was too late. Her physical and moral sufferings had brought her to the point of death.

CHAPTER NINE

BETWEEN DUTY AND DEVOTION

John VI having died in March, 1826, Dom Pedro suddenly found himself proclaimed King of Portugal and Algarve, as Pedro IV. Just as John had wished, the two kingdoms were now united under the scepter of his favorite son. A temporary regency presided over by the Princess Isabel-Maria had recognized the Emperor of Brazil as the legitimate sovereign, had had coins struck off bearing his effigy, and had dispatched an embassy headed by the Duke of Lafões to Rio de Janeiro to render him homage in behalf of the nation. Pedro, meanwhile, convinced that the union would be agreeable to neither of the two countries so long as he remained in Brazil, had decided to renounce the Portuguese crown in favor of his daughter, Maria da Gloria. Before he did so, however, he accepted the title of king, confirmed the regency, decreed a general amnesty, named seventy-seven peers, and granted the realm, which previously had been an absolute monarchy, a liberal constitution.

The news of this last-mentioned act burst like a bomb throughout the whole of Europe. Spain at once appealed to the allied powers, warning them of the danger to which she was exposed with liberalism entrenched on her frontiers. Nesselrode, speaking for Russia, declared that it was not possible to view the matter with indifference and that Brazil had cast upon Europe a firebrand that might end in a total conflagration. Metternich, for his part, inveighed against Dom Pedro's audacity, considering it "in the highest degree improper that a New World potentate should introduce a constitution into the Old World, turn a strict monarchy into a limited one." And he went on to assure Spain that "objective" measures would be taken against the Constitution at the least sign of a threat to the social peace of the Peninsula.

Only one voice on all the Continent was raised to applaud Dom Pedro's gesture—that of George Canning, who was looked upon by Metternich as being "the greatest rogue and liar in Europe, perhaps in the civilized world." In a speech in the House of Commons, in reply to a message of George IV, the great minister, speaking with emphasis and emotion, cried out: "May God prosper this attempt at constitutional liberty in Portugal!" In Portugal itself the constitution was to arouse tremendous opposition, beginning with the clergy, which was essentially conservative. The magistracy in turn prepared to put up a resistance, for the reason that the new principle of the division of powers threatened its income and its influence. But more decisive than anything else was the hostility of the lesser nobility. Living upon its country estates, it exerted a determining influence over the rural population. Banished from the Chamber of Peers, which was now reserved for dukes, counts, and marquises, and feeling that its wealth was threatened, it went over bag and baggage to join those who were opposed to the "Brazilian king."

Juridical arguments against Dom Pedro were promptly forthcoming. He could not inherit the crown for the reason that he was a foreigner, Brazil having already been recognized by Portugal as an empire. Moreover, as the absolutists pointed out, by the letters patent of 1642 the monarch was forbidden to reside outside the realm. As a consequence, Pedro could not confer upon Maria da Gloria a crown that did not belong to him; he could not give what he did not have. Therefore, let the succession pass to the second son, that is to say, to Dom Miguel.

At the time John VI died, Miguel had been living in exile in Vienna for nearly two years, as a result of having led an insurrection against his father, in April, 1824. A tool of his mother, whose daring and combativeness the years had not tempered, he had placed himself at the head of a body of troops and had attempted to seize control of the government. Thanks to the swift measures taken by the diplomatic corps, under the leadership of Hyde de Neuville, John was able to flee aboard the English ship *Windsor Castle,* and from there he had removed the prince from command of the army, compelling him to leave the country immediately.

It was Dom Pedro's idea that he could pacify Portugal by marrying his brother to the little princess Maria da Gloria (Maria II) as soon as she was old enough. Miguel fell in with this scheme readily enough, and on October 4, 1826, in the presence of the Portuguese minister at Vienna, he took the oath of allegiance to Pedro's constitution. Later appointed regent of Portugal during the queen's minority, he set out for Lisbon and assumed charge of the government, in February, 1828.

The gulf that had separated John VI from Dona Carlota was to be prolonged in the deep rift between Dom Pedro and Dom Miguel. His mother's obvious favorite, Miguel with the years had come to take on in her imagination the form of the archangel who was to avenge the affronts she had suffered and cleanse the Portuguese scepter of the mud of liberalism that clung to it, a liberalism which her husband had been too weak to oppose and which her first-born had aggravated by his senseless desertion of the royalist cause. Like the French legitimists, adherents of Louis XVIII and Charles X, who prided themselves on not having changed their ideas since 1789, Carlota was to die without having made the slightest concession to a liberal movement that was by

now triumphant. She had instilled in her son a mania for reaction;
she had drawn him into the restorationist adventure (the "April
coup") against his own father; with heavy heart and lips that
curled with hatred, she had seen him go into exile; and then for
long years she had waited with the consuming hope of seeing him
return with bared sword like another Gabriel to destroy the heretics
and Freemasons, after which, once his realm had been redeemed,
he would mount the throne beside her.

In order to hasten that moment she spared no sacrifice, was
deterred by no means however vile: bribery, poisoning—they
accused her of having done away with her husband—intrigue,
seduction, perfidy. What did it matter if Miguel lacked the gifts
of intelligence, decision, and a Machiavellian tact? She would
make up for it all with her diabolic cunning, her unshakable will,
her savage fanaticism, her arsenal of fencing tricks, with nothing
to restrain her but her own interests and the ends she sought. She
would be the brain, working behind him in the darkness; she
would be his inspiration. He would be the idol, the avenging
arm, the restorer of things as they were, the scourge of those who
had humiliated her. Even though belatedly, he would realize for
her the dreams that had not come true in life, and she would live
them now, by and through him and thanks to him.

Upon John's death Carlota had inherited 50,000,000 cruzados
in currency, 4,000,000 in gold,* and no telling how much in
Brazilian diamonds. With this money she would arrange for her
beloved Miguel to ascend the throne, she would buy up functionaries and judges, would pay off the Lisbon mob, the entire army
in fact, would fan the fanaticism of the friars, and start a conflagration in the provinces. She would have Friar John in his
sermons cry out in Miguel's presence: "My Lord, the Prince!
In the name of that God who is here present, in the name of reli-

* Approximately $250,000,000 and $450,000.

gion, I beg of you to put an end to this liberal riffraff made up of ungodly Freemasons. And I would have you know that there are three ways of doing so: by hanging them; by starving them to death in prison; and by giving them poison—poison, my Lord, poison!"

And thus it was that Dom Miguel found himself swept away by the torrent that was promptly unleashed upon his arrival. Transformed into a symbol rather than a party leader, he was irresistibly drawn into all sorts of mad acts. Bands of men armed with clubs now went through the streets beating up liberals under the tolerant gaze of the police even as Dom Pedro's leading sympathizers began leaving the country. It was impossible to stem the tide; and so he proceeded to dissolve the Congress, convoke the Three Estates, abolish the "Brazilian" Charter, and have himself crowned king.

This was a challenge to Dom Pedro, one that he would accept. Four years later the Brazilian monarch was to land in Portugal to resolve the matter as he was so fond of doing—with his own hands.

In addition to the events in Portugal which so preoccupied him, Pedro was also absorbed with the solution of another great external problem: the struggle for independence on the part of the Province of Cisplatina, today the Republic of Uruguay. This province was a legacy from the policy of John VI based upon natural boundaries. Ever since 1817, the peaceful-minded sovereign had maintained an occupation force in Montevideo, in order to keep watch on what went on in Buenos Aires on the other side of the River Plate. In 1821 the territory in question had been formally incorporated into Brazil and Uruguayan delegates had been sent to the assembly in Rio de Janeiro. This union, none the less, while it was regarded sympathetically by the educated

classes of Montevideo, was an artificial one and had against it
the record of three centuries of strife between Spain and Portugal.
Sooner or later an armed conflict was bound to break out, provoked
not only by the ambition of Buenos Aires to set up once more the
vice-royalty of the Plate River, but also by the spirit of independence of the majority of the inhabitants of the eastern
province.

Brazil, following the separation from Portugal, being busied
with the effort to organize the country, and having, in addition,
to face grave disturbances in the northern provinces, the Uru-
guayans sought to procure Argentine aid in shaking off the
imperial yoke. But the government of Buenos Aires was as yet
unprepared for the struggle, and not wishing to commit itself
prematurely, it confined its actions to requesting through
diplomatic channels the withdrawal of Brazilian troops from
Montevideo and the reincorporation of the territory with
Argentina, then the United Provinces of the River Plate. For a
number of months an Argentine envoy was in Rio for the purpose
of defending these claims; but his efforts were fruitless, and in
April, 1824, he returned home with a polite but categoric refusal
on the part of the Brazilian government.

The period of diplomatic negotiations having ended, the
Uruguyan patriots, led by Juan Antônio Lavalleja, then resorted
to action. On April 19, 1825, a spearhead of cavalry—the
"Immortal Thirty-Three"—crossed the Paraná River to begin a
guerrilla warfare against the occupation forces. From Argentina
arms, munitions, and other supplies were arriving in ever increasing quantities for the liberation groups, which were rapidly
multiplying throughout the province. With the Brazilian forces
idling in their garrisons, Lavalleja was able to convoke a congress
in the city of Florida, and in August the delegates voted for the
reincorporation of Uruguay with Argentina, declaring null and

void all previous treaties with Portugal and with Brazil. This news, together with the favorable result of the first encounters with the imperial units, evoked an enormous enthusiasm throughout Argentina, silencing the opposition and unifying the public opinion of the nation around the government's foreign policy. In October the Congress of Buenos Aires agreed to the incorporation of Uruguay.

For Brazil there remained no other recourse than war. A fleet under the command of Admiral Rodrigo Lobo was sent to blockade the River Plate, and the Brazilian commander in Uruguay, General Lecor, received orders to take the offensive on land. The admiral, unlike his men, was lacking in the necessary aggressiveness, and his deep-sea craft proved inadequate for navigating the comparatively shallow waters of the estuary. And Lecor, with army morale greatly relaxed as a result of long years of inactivity, did not deploy his troops as he should have done. The result was that the insurrection spread without hindrance. His mind being taken up with political matters, the attempt to consolidate the monarchy and to subject the northern provinces to the central authority, Dom Pedro had not given the proper attention to the struggle in the south. As a result, the ranks were thin and the men were ill fed, ill paid, worse mounted, and almost in rags. England, in the meantime, was endeavoring to obstruct in every way it could Brazilian action along the River Plate. Canning's plan was to make of Montevideo a sort of Hanseatic city under a British protectorate. An able politician, the great minister thought to accomplish through political shrewdness what Sir Horne Popham had failed to achieve by force in 1806; namely, the establishment in the River Plate region of an English naval base for the South Atlantic.

With conditions growing worse and the maritime blockade proving ineffective while at the same time giving rise to daily conflicts with European powers whose commerce was affected, the emperor decided to set out for the south in order personally to investigate the needs of his troops, reorganize them, and himself lead them on the field of battle. Three weeks previously he had sent ahead to the front as the new commander-in-chief the marquis of Barbacena, one of the outstanding figures of the empire, a broad-visioned diplomat and statesman and a great organizer, though not a professional soldier.

Dom Pedro's departure coincided with a serious crisis through which the empress was passing. She was still wasting away with melancholy, and the prospect of being separated from her husband merely increased her depression, filling her with cares and forebodings. It was necessary, however, that he leave at once. The Argentine and Uruguayan forces were already threatening the frontiers of Rio Grande do Sul, and only through the emperor's presence would it be possible to organize the defense of the province and launch a counteroffensive.

On the afternoon of November 24, 1826, at the head of a fleet consisting of ten naval units, Dom Pedro sailed out of Guanabara Bay. Upon his departure, Leopoldina had given him as a token of love and friendship a symbolic ring. It held two diamonds, and on the inside of the band were two hearts and two names. She was tormented by a gloomy presentiment that she would never see her husband again, and his name, tenderly whispered, was to be constantly on her lips until a deep and invincible torpor came to close her eyes in death: "My Pedro, my dear Pedro . . ."

On the 30th of November, the emperor disembarked at the port of Santa Catarina, and by the following day he was already off for Porto Alegre, capital of the province of Rio Grande do Sul. In spite of all his worries—in addition to the state of Leopoldina's health, the opposition to his government was growing stronger day by day—Dom Pedro gave himself over unreservedly to the task of raising the morale of the troops. He reduced to the ranks those officers who were too much concerned with nonmilitary matters, intensified the recruiting, trained the men who were called to the colors, shook the rear-guard garrisons out of their lethargy, computed the forces at his command, located supply depots, and mapped out the operations that were to come. To the viscount of São Leopoldo, correspondents in the south wrote: "His Majesty's presence is worth more than an army!" They were right about that. The natives of Rio Grande, who previously had done everything they could to avoid being drafted and by their passivity had delayed the carrying out of military orders, were now suddenly enthusiastic for the campaign. Confidence had been reborn. The officers being better aware of their duties and the soldiers having been paid off, the army began to lose the aspect of a mere aggregation of Negroes, Germans, Indians, Portuguese, and half-breeds.

Barely three weeks had gone by, spent in this sort of activity, when a special messenger arrived at Porto Alegre, bringing news of the court. One of the letters was from Friar Antônio de Arrabida, and as Dom Pedro read it, his heart beat rapidly: "My pen, even, refuses to write the words! The virtuous Empress Leopoldina no longer is of this world!"

There were other letters that provided him with the details of what had occurred. On the morning of the 2nd of December, the empress had aborted a masculine fetus. For many days afterward she ran a high fever which the palace physicians were unable to bring down. On the fourth, her condition appeared to improve and she made a confession and received the Sacrament; but immediately afterward she began to have hallucinations and fainting spells, to suspect the medicines that were given her, and to behold terrifying visions. The Marchioness of Santos and the Duchess of Goiaz suddenly filled her with horror; she refused to see them, and in her delirium attributed to them the powers of black magic. They then had to ask Domitila not to enter the room where Leopoldina was suffering her last agony, the result of an incurable puerperal septicemia.

On December 6th, one of his ministers, the Marquis of Paranaguá, addressed these frank words to Dom Pedro: "I ought not to conceal from Your Imperial Majesty the fact that the people are murmuring, and greatly, regarding the origin of the affection, choosing to attribute it to moral rather than to physical causes." On the morning of the 11th, Leopoldina died in the arms of the royal chaplain. They all kissed the hand of the corpse and then conveyed the remains in a triple casket to the Ajuda Convent. And even as the bells were tolling mournfully, the whisper spread abroad that the marchioness had conspired with the court physician to poison the empress and that her little son Pedro had been substituted for the real crown prince.[1]

Stunned by the news, the emperor at once abandoned all his military projects and galloped away at top speed over the coastal sands in the direction of the port of Santa Catarina. No sooner had the ship put in to take him aboard than he gave the order to depart, without even allowing time to lay in a stock of provisions, the crew being forced to subsist on minimum rations of water, rice, and salt beef. At a distance of less than thirty miles from Guanabara Bay, in the vicinity of Sepetiba, he grew impatient over the calm that was holding up the boat and insisted upon being lowered into a sloop that he might be rowed ashore. It was necessary for the ship's captain to say to him: "I am the one who is responsible for Your Majesty's life, and since I am in command here, I will not permit them to lower a boat!" [2]

In the south, Barbacena was left with the overwhelming task of preparing for the imminent combat with the republican troops. On the morning of the 20th of February (1827), the patrols of Alvear's army encountered the first Brazilian outposts, near Passo do Rosario. The Argentineans, some twelve thousand men in all, had facing them a force of less than seven thousand, led by Barbacena and José de Abreu, Baron of Serro Largo. The latter having been shot down in the vanguard position he had claimed for himself, his cavalry battalions broke up; and had it not been for the infantry, which obstinately stood its ground, the Brazilian would have been completely routed. After eleven hours of fighting, the imperial troops started moving northward and the Argentineans toward Corrales. Although the Brazilians had lost only 120 men as against the enemy's 500, the honors of the day went to the republicans for their valor and fighting spirit. On the other hand, so far as practical results were concerned, the imperials seemingly had the better of it, in view of the fact that the enemy, which had been fighting on Brazilian territory, had once more been driven back across the frontier. It is for this reason that the battle in question, which took place more than one hundred years ago, still remains to be decided.

There followed a period of stagnation in the front lines, broken only by skirmishes of no significance. The United Provinces were militarily and financially exhausted, without the means of carrying on the war. In Buenos Aires, President Dorrego exclaimed: "In the armory there is not a single bullet to fire against the enemy. I have done what I could to remedy matters, but there is not a rifle, not a bit of powder, nor any money with which to buy munitions!" Under such conditions Don Manuel Garcia, himself, minister of foreign affairs of the United Provinces, set out for Rio de Janeiro to negotiate a peace at any price. On May 24, 1827, a treaty was signed in accordance with the terms of which the Argentineans were to evacuate Cisplatina and recognize that region as being a province of the Brazilian Empire.

In Buenos Aires, however, feeling ran too high for them to accept an unconditional surrender. The reaction, indeed, was so intense that the government ended by disavowing its own minister and rejecting the treaty. This news caused great dismay in Rio. Although finances were not at as low an ebb here as in Argentina, Brazil nevertheless was at grips with tremendous budgetary problems. The campaign was an unpopular one, being regarded as contrary to the spirit of the country, and in all classes of society the Uruguayan patriots did not lack their partisans and sympathizers. Volunteers were scarce and public dissatisfaction with the war was becoming more widespread every day. And then England and France, whose commerce had been seriously impaired by the blockade, began exerting pressure for a cessation of hostilities. On the 27th of August the definitive peace treaty was signed. Brazil and Argentina were both to give up their claims to sovereignty over Cisplatina and recognize its independence. And it was on this date that the Republic of Uruguay took its place in the family of nations.

No happier a solution could have been found. This territory, a kind of South American Alsace-Lorraine, thereby ceased to be a center of discord, to become the permanent basis of equilibrium in the River Plate basin.

Dom Pedro had never loved Leopoldina. He had, however, grown so attached to her in the course of the years that her death left an enormous void in his life. He had become accustomed to seeing her playing with the children, a good and simple creature always ready to forgive his excesses and indiscretions, and a loyal counselor in time of trouble, magnetized by his rude tyranny. The thought that by flaunting his adultery he might possibly have shortened her days was like a hot iron applied to his heedless yet sensitive heart. Upon his return from the south, suffering deeply, he did not wish to see anyone and was ill tempered toward courtiers, ministers, and even the marchioness herself. After six months his attitude had changed but little. At a banquet in commemoration of St. Isabella's day, he suddenly noticed that the table was spread on the exact spot where Leopoldina's body had lain in state. Overcome with a strange emotion, he left the room; when at length he did not return, Domitila went to look for him. She found him in one of the chambers of the palace, with tears in his eyes, embracing the portrait of his dead wife.

Some nights before, impetuously, like one possessed, he had torn himself from the marchioness's arms: "Let me go! I know that the life I am leading is one unworthy of a sovereign. The thought of the empress will not leave me." He was gnawed by a cruel remorse at having requited her great love with indifference, her fidelity with adultery, her tenderness with harshness, her loyalty with treason. He felt himself guilty, felt like a hangman, the executioner of an innocent being whose life he had consciously and unfeelingly embittered: he had deprived her of her illusions, her happiness, and in the end—who could say?—of life itself, perhaps. The sonnet that he composed for her (verses seemed to come to him in these tragic hours) is the cry of a lost soul:

> Eternal God, why hast Thou taken from me
> My Empress whom I loved so well?

Meanwhile, political intrigues, the murmurings of nobles in corners of the palace, their sullen looks, the conspiracies that he sensed were afoot, and the heavily laden atmosphere of Rio de Janeiro all tended to show him the gravity of the situation. The hostility between the emperor and the Congress was now entering upon its critical phase. The clashes between the executive and legislative branches, as might be expected in a country in which constitutional and parliamentary government were still a novelty, were aggravated by Dom Pedro's domineering temperament as well as by the eagerness of certain congressional leaders to bring about the faultless functioning of cabinet government.

The emperor's dissolute life; the lowly origin of some of his most intimate friends and advisers; the terms of the Luso-Brazilian Treaty of 1825, which were considered excessively favorable to Portugal; and finally, the peace treaty with Argentina, granting independence to Uruguay—these were the favorite themes on which the parliamentary opposition loved to harp. But in reality, everything was due to one original sin on Dom Pedro's part, that of having been born in Portugal. Let him show the least tolerance for Portuguese citizens or interests, and he was at once accused of partisanship, of leaning more toward Portugal than toward his adopted country. He had given Brazil its liberty; by his presence, he had assured national unity; he had granted the country a constitution of a kind for which the older peoples of Europe were still to do battle; but the emperor's enemies in their excitement forgot all this and, misrepresenting the pure and unstinted love he bore the country, proceeded to heap the most unjust suspicions upon his head.

In Portugal, on the other hand, they could not forgive Dom Pedro for the crime of having favored the separation of Brazil, and sought to compel the aged John to disinherit him and strip him of his nationality. Unsuccessful in this, they were later to deny him the right of succession to the throne and of abdicating in favor of his daughter. Portuguese tradition, they cried out, had always repudiated "foreign" kings. In Brazil, such is the logic of human ingratitude, they did not want him because he was Portuguese, and in Portugal they refused to have him because he was Brazilian.

Since Dom Pedro with his military inclinations was in constant contact with the troops, reviewing their exercises and frequently taking part in them, the army became suspect to the Congress, which sought to weaken it in every possible way. This was one of the principal reasons for that lack of preparedness with which Brazil had had to face the war in the south. Dom Pedro, after his own manner, returned the attacks that were made upon him, as when he leaned from a window facing the Chamber of Deputies to hurl insults at the members of the Congress as they passed. At the close of each legislative session, it was customary for the emperor to deliver an address summing up what had been accomplished; but in 1830 there existed so much ill will on both sides that he decided to make his speech a short one—short and cutting: "Most worthy representatives of the nation, the session is closed."

Dom Miguel having taken possession of the Portuguese throne and begun a large-scale persecution of liberals and of Dona Maria da Gloria's followers, many of these fled for refuge to London or to Brazil. As the father and guardian of the young queen, Pedro could not hold himself aloof from these events nor avoid the involvement, at least indirectly, of Brazilian interests; and this was yet another weapon in the hands of his adversaries, who reproached him for his intimacy with Portuguese subjects and the small concern he showed for Brazilian problems.

On August 13, 1827, Domitila gave birth to a girl baby, her third offspring by Dom Pedro. The child was named Maria-Isabel and received, with its first wails, the title of Duchess of Ceará.

The impulsive young man of twenty-nine was coming of age. The situation of Brazil, the upsurge of the republican and anarchistic spirit, the future of the American dynasty: all these problems he envisaged with a kind of crude clarity. For the first time he was feeling the full weight of the responsibilities that rested upon his shoulders. In his hands lay the destiny of his descendants, heirs to the throne of Brazil. He might give them a well organized and happy land over which to rule, or he might pass on to them a tottering crown with the prospect of downfall and a melancholy exile. He accordingly decided to begin reforming his life by restoring the imperial dignity. Conceiving a plan to marry again, he suddenly broke off relations with the marchioness. "He does not see her any more," the Prussian representative in Rio informed his government, "despite all the efforts that she has made to get him to do so." But the birth of Maria-Isabel shook his firm resolve to a certain extent. He could not resist having a look, sooner or later, at the little one who, after all, was his own flesh and blood, a part of his life; and so, risking the reputation he was trying so hard to rebuild, he furtively stole through his mistress's doorway to satisfy the desire he could not resist, of bending over the cradle of the newborn.

His father-in-law, the Emperor of Austria, had given him a bit of "fatherly advice" to the effect that he ought to contract another marriage, and at the same time had proffered his own good offices. Acting upon this counsel, Pedro forwarded to Vienna the documents necessary for the conclusion of the matter; and on the 19th of August, even as Maria-Isabel was being christened, the Marquis of Barbacena set out for Europe for the purpose of completing negotiations and bringing the bride back to Rio. Months before, in ending a letter to the marchioness, the emperor had intertwined his name with that of Domitila and had added a postscript: "Thus shall we always be; whatever may happen in the world, nothing shall ever part us." It was love that spoke then; but the hour of duty was soon to come when he would coolly sacrifice upon the altar of present needs the amorous devotion of yesterday.

CHAPTER TEN

THE EMPEROR HUNTS A WIFE

The French Revolution and the Napoleonic Empire, after twenty years of warfare, had left Europe in a state of exhaustion. Never before in history had there been such striking and profound changes in the political map of the Continent. Each charge of grenadiers had traced new frontiers for the various peoples. There were two tasks which the allied monarchs had set themselves in their effort to recompose the Continent. One, of a political nature, consisted in bringing about a balance of power; this was the task of the Congress of Vienna. The other, an ideological one, had to do with stopping the spread of revolutionary ideas, which was the objective of the Holy Alliance.

The one who furnished the inspiration and intellectual guidance in connection with both these tasks was the Austrian chancellor, Prince Klemens Wenzel Nepomuk Lothar von Metternich. At the age of twenty, Metternich had declared war on the new and revolutionary ideas. As a student in Strasbourg and Mainz, he had witnessed the beginnings of the tragedy that had brought shipwreck to the France of the Bourbons. Watching the mob that sacked the Strasbourg prefecture, he had come to know the tremendous, wild, fanatic strength that lay in these new concepts which were an outstanding danger to the social peace of the world; and from then on he had definitely foreseen his future role: that of defending with all his energies the sociopolitical heritage of humanity against these forces that had been unleashed by fanaticism and the spirit of revolt.

From there he went on to action. On the day following Marie Antoinette's execution, he drew up a ringing "Appeal to the Army," and shortly afterward he published a small tract *On the Necessity of Arming the People on the French Frontiers, by a Friend of Public Order*. In Strasbourg M. Koch had taught him that "the system of a balance of power for more than three centuries has been the cornerstone of all European politics." He was never to forget that lesson. As soon as one power began arming itself unduly, the master would explain, and aspired to hegemony, all the others, impelled by an instinct of solidarity and self-preservation, must unite to defend the higher interests of the European community. Guided by this way of thinking, the pupil was later to draw up plans for those anti-French coalitions with which he was to combat and bring to naught Napoleon's ambitions.

Now, Metternich was not, spiritually speaking, an Austrian. It was less out of love for Austria than out of devotion to his political ideals that he gave himself body and soul to the furtherance of the Hapsburg Empire. A mystic at heart, in all he did he was simply being loyal to those principles of which he had made himself the guardian. German historians, for whom history is a doctrinaire matter, have never forgiven him for the obstacles he put in the way of German unification. He combated Prussian expansion with the same inflexibility with which he imposed on France the frontiers of 1789. A European citizen, "God's lieutenant," he worked for the Hapsburgs in order to serve Europe, which was his true fatherland. He once confessed to Wellington: "For a long time Europe has had for me the significance of a fatherland."

Napoleon had left in his wake, in all countries, the seed of revolution, and it was necessary to destroy this subtle threat in order that the social equilibrium of each state might be maintained. This internal equilibrium, as the great chancellor saw it, was the indispensable basis for any continental balance of power. Alongside the great masses of the people, who were passively conformist in tendency, there was a militant minority that was animated by a new spirit and that ardently aspired to political and religious freedom. From 1815 to 1848 the struggle was to go on incessantly between the old regime and its liberal enemies.

Exaggeratedly susceptible to any kind of mysticism, Czar Alexander was convinced that the Almighty had chosen him to lay down a new law for Europe. Believing that his mission was "to substitute in all public relations the principles of the Gospel of Christ for the evil traditions of Machiavellian statecraft," he made ready to formulate the bases of a *Weltanschauung* that should mark the luminous resurgence of the Christian theocracy of the Middle Ages. With his allies, the Emperor of Austria and the King of Prussia, he proceeded to sign the famous pact that came to be known as the Holy Alliance, "in the Name of the Most Holy and Indivisible Trinity."

Even though the Alliance impressed him as being "a loud-sounding nothing," Metternich resolved to transform it into a true syndicate of kings, directed against the liberal movements. The first step lay in an appeal to the political police, his plan being to coordinate the police of all the states for common action and to support them in moments of crisis with the armed forces of the powers. This was, clearly, the *right of intervention*. When a power was unable by its own means to put down the revolutionary ferment, the others should intervene to guarantee the existence of the legitimate authority. With this weapon Metternich was to crush the young liberal movements of Germany,

Naples, the Piedmont, the Two Sicilies, and Spain, composed of those who were fascinated by the mirage of constitutional government.

Dom Pedro of Brazil was to become the most dangerous enemy of this "system." No one else, the chancellor complained, had done so much harm to the Holy Alliance as had the son-in-law of His Apostolic Majesty. He would never be able to understand, much less justify, the conduct of a sovereign who had joined with Carbonari and who had disdained the prerogatives of "divine right" to grant *of his own free will* libertarian constitutions. He could understand how Napoleon, a lucky upstart adventurer, might trample European traditions underfoot, but it appeared to him inconceivable that Pedro, a prince of the blood and heir to one of the oldest dynasties, should imitate the Corsican and make a mockery of age-old principles, and all because he had a mad obsession for granting charters.

When Dom Pedro asked the emperor of Austria to arrange a second marriage for him, he forgot that behind the throne of the Hapsburgs lurked the clever, crafty figure of Metternich, only waiting for a chance to retaliate for the "sacrilege" of which the Brazilian monarch had been guilty.

To begin with, a second marriage for Pedro was not likely to be agreeable to Austria. If he were to have more sons, they would occupy the thrones of Brazil and Portugal, in case other heirs to those crowns were lacking, to the prejudice of the daughters of the first marriage bed. It was obviously to the emperor of Austria's interest that these countries should be governed by his grandchildren rather than by princes of other royal houses, who might possibly be opposed to Austrian policy. This drawback, however, might readily have been overcome by Metternich; all he would have had to do would have been to arrange a match with one of the Bavarian princesses who, to judge by those who were already married, were all of them sterile. But no, Metternich could not let slip this opportunity of avenging himself on the royal "Freemason" who had almost brought about the downfall of "his" (Metternich's) system by an untimely desertion of the cause of kings. What he wished to do was inflict upon him a prolonged humiliation in all the courts of the world by seeing to it that the successive overtures that were made for the hands of a dozen European princesses were repelled, one by one.

The Brazilian negotiators were none too capable, and the unsavory reputation that Dom Pedro enjoyed in Europe fitted in marvelously well with the chancellor's designs. He knew that the refusal of a princess's hand in marriage meant for a monarch a great blow to his dignity. He was aware that in transactions of this sort the formal request is only made after it is known that the prospective bride and her family are favorably disposed. He also knew perfectly well that in such matters absolute secrecy is indispensable to a successful outcome in order that those interests that might be harmed by the projected alliance may not have a chance to summon their forces to stop it, or to put difficulties in the way. But Metternich gloried in systematically violating such simple and readily understood principles as these. Was not he the one who dictated court etiquette and ceremonial and who handled the affairs of Austria with so much refined formality and circumspection?

So he permitted matters to take their course, with plans being laid and certain princesses being approached of whose refusal he was certain in advance, if indeed he himself was not responsible for it. On the other hand, he allowed the journals and gazettes of all Europe to fill their columns with calumnies and insults to Dom Pedro as they reprinted the gossip concerning the empress's death and depicted the court of Rio de Janeiro as being a luxurious brothel from which the Marchioness of Santos governed, to suit her whims, a huge American empire. Whenever negotiations were begun in a certain quarter, notices of this sort would increase as if by magic, filling the princess in the case with horror for this American sultan who was in the habit of assassinating his wives and transforming the imperial palace into a bordello.

When the Neapolitan minister, the Prince of Cassaro, attempted to arrange a match with a member of his own royal house, Metternich was furious. What business had the diplomat intruding on these preserves? How dare he even think of such a thing without precise instructions to that effect? Let him not meddle in matters that did not concern him.

In view of these successive and resounding failures Dom Pedro grew impatient, and the Marquis of Barbacena began to suspect that there was a plot to prevent the emperor of Brazil from marrying again. Writing to his sovereign from Vienna on February 13, 1828, the envoy added to his letter a separate note written in code: "Secret. Suspect treachery to keep you from having more children. Do not give the least indication of this as I expect to get at the truth of the matter within a week." Following the example of the Marquis of Resende, who gave costly presents to the wives of influential men and lined with gold the pockets of Viennese functionaries, Barbacena discreetly handed out large sums to two persons to whom he "made himself agreeable in a manner which they could not resist." One of these was on terms of greatest intimacy with the chancellor while the other occupied a leading post in his cabinet, and hence was in a position to find out what there was to the conjectures.

Prince Metternich was, as a matter of fact, holding up the negotiations and took a secret delight in doing so; but venality was rife among the leading figures of Viennese society, and when Resende ceremoniously undertook to bribe Gentz with expensive gifts, that great diplomat smiled and at once put him perfectly at his ease: "I do not know that, strictly speaking, I really ought to accept any gift; but of one thing I can assure you, and that is that I always prefer gold ingots (*des lingots d'or*) to any other remuneration whatsoever."

Clever and ingratiating, Barbacena even tried to get into the good graces of Metternich's mother-in-law, "a woman who was very indiscreet and communicative," in order that he might win her confidence and obtain the information that he needed. Ingeniously humoring Baroness von Leykam's excessive talkativeness, he succeeded in leading her on to reveal her son-in-law's schemes; for this excellent lady ardently desired to obtain the intercession of the Emperor of Brazil in connection with certain matters in which her husband was interested. Availing himself of this circumstance, the marquis always replied that the favor she sought would be granted just as soon as the marriage had been arranged. Growing more impatient all the while, the baroness finally told him: "Metternich will never provide a stepmother for his sovereign's granddaughters; you may as well go about it some other way."

Breaking off negotiations, Pedro wrote to his father-in-law "not to continue courting refusals" and called Barbacena back to Rio for fresh instructions. The marquis remained in Brazil less than two months, and on July 4 (1828) sailed for Europe again to renew the hunt for a bride. The emperor's instructions were: "My great desire is to procure a princess who by reason of her birth, beauty, virtue, and education shall bring happiness to me and to the empire; if possible, I should like her to combine the four qualities mentioned, but if any of them are to be dispensed with, let it be the first and the last, as I must insist upon the second and the third."

In the meantime, Metternich, betraying the good faith of the

Brazilian minister in Vienna, had seen to it that Dom Pedro was repulsed once more, and most spectacularly. The Austrian chancellor had ended by convincing the Marquis of Resende that if he wished the glory of obtaining an empress for Brazil, he ought to apply to the Prince of Sweden for the hand of his sister. "The prince," Barbacena afterward related, "pretended to accept the offer and let it become known to the Emperor of Austria, whereupon the entire diplomatic corps became aware of it; and there was poor Resende betaking himself to Karlsruhe on the day specified and at the appointed hour to make the formal request of the princess herself, only to receive from her a round No, a fact which Metternich took care to have published in all the gazettes."

Forty-eight hours before, Prince Gustave had received a courier from Vienna.

Learning, upon his arrival at Gibraltar, of the Princess Cecilia's refusal, Barbacena hastened to write the emperor, remarking that this "merely serves to convince the most incredulous of Metternich's perfidy; far from arranging a marriage for Your Majesty, he has been the most energetic in preventing it." And he went on to pose the question: "Who in his right senses would ever believe that the daughter of a dethroned king" (Princess Cecilia of Sweden was the daughter of Gustavus Adolphus who had been unseated in 1890) "and who lives as best she can, entirely dependent upon the Austrian Empire, would refuse the hand of the Emperor of Brazil, unless she had been obliged to do so by the Austrian cabinet?" As he saw it, the only solution was to look for a princess outside Vienna's sphere of influence. "In London," he wrote, "I shall be able to find out exactly what is going on in this regard; and while the Austrians suppose that my attention is wholly absorbed with the affairs of Portugal and with preparations for my journey to Vienna, I shall be able to arrange a marriage for Your Majesty with some princess who is not under their domination, and this without giving them time for any intrigues."

Meanwhile, efforts made in Denmark had not been any more fortunate in their outcome. Barbacena had dispatched an envoy to Copenhagen whose duty it was to gather exact data regarding the physical and moral endowments of the Danish princess, the king's niece. Without so much as having seen her and relying merely upon hearsay, the Brazilian representative made the proper overtures, and greatly encouraged by this, Barbacena wrote long and hopeful letters to the emperor. Disillusionment, however, was not slow in coming, leaving the envoy "with a face that would scare a child from the breast," to quote the Marquis of Resende's words. For more accurate information had arrived from Copenhagen than that which the plenipotentiary had transmitted to Rio:

I now know that the princess is, true enough, an elegant young lady; but her eyes, eyelids, and eyebrows are those of an albino, as is the case with all the princesses of that country, which is enough to render even the greatest beauty in the world repulsive-looking. Albinos are what we in Brazil call "high yellows," or octoroons, and would Your Imperial Majesty care for such a bride as that? Certainly not. I therefore shall let matters drop in this quarter and carry on elsewhere.

Resende, on the other hand, had already sent the emperor the most gratifying reports. "Louisa is the name of Your Majesty's future bride," he had written triumphantly, "a lady who morally and physically is bound to please Your Majesty. I am one who has cut an unhappy figure where marriage is concerned, but in this case I shall do everything that lies within my power." His optimism, indeed, was something quite out of the ordinary. Whenever fresh negotiations were begun, he would write the emperor in a burst of enthusiasm: "I have found at last an illustrious, beautiful, young, and highly accomplished bride for Your Majesty!" And when news came of the refusal, he would vent his verbal wrath upon the Viennese diplomats: "Austrian bedbugs," "southern devils," "Jesuits of the first water"!

The emperor's impatience reached a high point when, on January 15, 1829, Mareschal sought him out to hand him a letter from Metternich in which that minister begged a thousand pardons for not having been able to arrange the marriage as yet and repeated the same old stories of constant failure. And when the Austrian representative showed him two portraits, one of the Princess Cecilia, and the other of the Princess Louisa, Dom Pedro, losing his composure, replied that this was "the crowning outrage and villainy on the part of the crafty Metternich, sending him these two portraits—which certainly differed from the originals—just to obtain his good will in matters pertaining to Portugal." Then, working himself up into a rage, he went on to shout at the astounded diplomat:

"Metternich is becoming all the time more hateful and shameless. Send those portraits back to him and tell him that anything that comes from him is not worthy of being viewed by me. As for the marriage, that is all over, so far as Metternich or the Austrian court or any other court is concerned!"

Metternich interpreted this explosion on Dom Pedro's part as indicating that he was giving up the fight. The chancellor felt that he had scored a victory, but he was very much mistaken. Even as the diplomats were idling, giving the Austrian minister the impression that nothing was being done, other intermediaries were quietly at work arranging the second marriage. At one point Metternich got wind of the proceedings and forthwith unleashed a most violent campaign against Dom Pedro, the papers being filled once more with slanders and defamations, including the "news" that the emperor's marriage with the marchioness of Santos had already taken place. It was too late, however. On the 2nd of August in Munich, the marriage of the Brazilian sovereign to Amelia Napoleon of Leuchtenberg was consummated. His Apostolic Majesty's invincible minister had suffered a defeat for once. Nevertheless, up to the last moment the Brazilians were afraid that Metternich might upset everything. Barbacena had written from London: "It is possible that he will undo this, but we either have to give up the idea of marrying off the emperor during Metternich's lifetime, or else take some risk."

Antonio Fortunato Brack, lieutenant colonel of the Napoleonic guard, had discovered in Bavaria the loveliest and most charming offspring that the Germanic race could show. Sailing for Brazil, he had revealed his plan to Dom Pedro and had returned to Europe furnished with a special set of instructions. The bride not only combined those two essential requisites that the emperor had demanded, beauty and virtue; there was an additional circumstance that was very significant: she belonged to a house that was traditionally hostile to Metternich. Thus the blow would be all the more effective and Dom Pedro's triumph the more complete. Resende's enthusiasm upon seeing Princess Amelia knew no bounds. In his picturesque style he described her for his sovereign as possessing "an airy body such as that which the painter Correggio in his pictures bestows upon the Queen of Sheba, and an affability that melts the hearts of all who know her; upon returning home I had to exclaim, 'By the five wounds of Our Lord, Jesus Christ, sinner that I am, why am not I the Emperor of Brazil?' "

Dom Pedro later was to be thankful for the successive refusals that he had received. More lovely and enchanting than all the princesses whose hands he had sought, Amelia represented for him conjugal bliss at the very moment when he thought it utterly unattainable. Tired of waiting and hurt by the humiliations which the European courts had inflicted upon him, he might, with his uncontrollable temperament, have rushed into any form of excess, including a marriage with Domitila and a breaking off of relations with Europe. He had been saved from that.

CHAPTER ELEVEN

OFF WITH THE OLD LOVE

Parting from Domitila was not an easy matter. In order to flee the temptation of seeing her, Dom Pedro spent long periods on his Santa Cruz plantation, in the company of all his children, including the young Duchess of Goiaz. As for the little Maria-Isabel, on the day following her baptism she had been taken into the palace, where four nurses were assigned to look after her.

In September (1827) the monarch weakened, and under that date we have a note of his addressed to the marchioness: "Good-by, my dear girl, until eleven o'clock, when I shall be there without fail to enjoy the greatest pleasure that I know, that of embracing you." Shortly afterward he recovered his self-control, only to fall again later on. In December he is grave and formal: "My dear Marchioness, I should like to hear how you are getting along and let you know that the children are in good health. Please accept my assurance of the purest, most sincere, and *proper* friendship on the part of him who so esteems you and who is your Emperor." A short while later, having perhaps been invited to come and see her, he recapitulates the reasons for their separation, and concludes: "This leads me once more to protest my love for you, but at the same time I must tell you that I cannot come."

In the beginning of 1828 the notes are more frequent, revealing always a special interest in Domitila's health: "I have been very much worried about you ever since last night, when they told me that you thought you might be coming down with a fever; that is something that does not surprise me, knowing as I do how careless you are about eating and still more so about drafts." On the same day (February 6th) he writes her again: "I am very glad to know that there is nothing wrong with you and that you are in good health, but I trust you will not fail to observe that dependable rule of our ancestors, who were so much wiser in such matters than we: one day of convalescence for every day of illness." And a little later: "I should like very much to know if the dampness isn't bad for you when you leave the theater in a carriage without curtains."

Word from Europe to the effect that his marriage could not be consummated so long as the marchioness remained in Rio irritated the emperor and led him to interrupt the pleasant tone of his letters by reproaching her: "It was not without good reason that I advised you, under pretext of your health, to ask my permission to go and reside in some other province of the empire so that the arrangements for my marriage might be completed." Further on, he even fixes the precise date: "It is absolutely necessary for you to leave this month or by the middle of next, at the latest." Displeased at this, Domitila replied: "My presence ought not to be annoying to Your Majesty, whether you are getting married or not getting married"; but she finally did return to São Paulo, her native province, from which she had emerged to live her much talked of and tempestuous romance.

The emperor was unable to put the favorite out of his mind, the sacrifice appearing to him at times more than he had the strength to bear. Before the marchioness had reached São Paulo, he was already writing to remind her that, a few days later, they would have completed six years of life in common: "I certainly hope that you will be happy and that all will go well with you, and I trust you will always remember the 29th, that day on which all our troubles began as a consequence of our meeting for the first time—how happy we were then, today how sad!" [1] And he continued: "But what am I saying? I have only myself to blame and can but bless the happy time that I have spent with you. Ah, my girl, what love for you exists within this heart of mine— *your* heart—being held in check only by my honor and the necessity of keeping my word!" Finally, he makes a timid and naïve request of her: "Remember me always and (forgive me) do not look at anyone else; it is enough that I have done you wrong."

Two months later, in the palace at São Cristovão, the little Maria-Isabel, Duchess of Ceará, died of meningitis after having lain in convulsions for forty hours. The profound grief which the loss of their daughter caused him brought him close to the marchioness once more, and she replied to his letters: "I am certain that you will want to see me very soon; you may believe me when I say that I am devoured by impatience, for I am slowly pining away."

The month of April witnessed Domitila's triumphal return. Having been informed of her departure, the emperor set out from Santa Cruz to meet her in Jaguaí. "During the first days of her restoration to favor, she has given the most striking proof of the boundless credit she enjoys at court." Such was the word which the diplomats hastened to send back to their respective courts. There was an insistent rumor in Rio to the effect that, disillusioned in his attempt to find a European princess, Dom Pedro was to marry the marchioness and that she first of all was to be elevated to the highest rank of the imperial nobility. Baron Olfers, the Prussian ambassador, on this point was emphatic in his dispatches: "She is aiming at marriage and at the throne." In the meanwhile, nothing is known for a certainty as to just what it was that prevented Domitila's marriage and coronation. It is an open question as to whether it was the threat to assassinate her that had been made by a senator, Diogo Antônio Feijó, or a withdrawal on the part of Dom Pedro, who had come to his senses in time; or it may be that the favorite herself, inspired by patriotism, was led to sacrifice her love to the security and well-being of the empire, and had refused him.

The 24th of May was marked by an impressive event that was quite out of the ordinary. In her handsome carriage, drawn by six horses with liveried grooms, the marchioness arrived at the São Cristovão palace for the afternoon reception. She wore an embroidered cloak adorned with plumes and precious stones, and about her throat was a beautiful gold necklace from which hung the emperor's portrait framed in diamonds. Between rows of guardsmen in full dress, lined up with their halberds and rapiers, Domitila mounted the grand staircase and was conducted by chamberlains into the presence of Dom Pedro and the children, among them the Duchess of Goiaz. The marchioness kissed her daughter on the face and put her lips to the emperor's hand as he stood there, a magnificent figure in his gold lace and insignia, after which she kissed the hands of the princesses, who also were luxuriously attired. The lovers thereupon exchanged a few ceremonious words and Domitila extended an invitation to the emperor to have a cup of tea at her house that night. Dom Pedro accepted and, breaking all the rules of etiquette, accompanied her to the top of the outside stair.

By eight o'clock he was at the door of the mansion in the rua Nova, where a distinguished group of guests was waiting to receive him. Extending his right hand for the lips of his vassals, the emperor jovially put them all at their ease by saying: *"Sans façon, en liberté."* After a splendid supper had been served, Dom Pedro and the marchioness began the formal square dances, impeccable quadrilles performed under the watchful eye of dancing master Louis Lacombe. In the course of the evening cooling drinks were circulated, dainty edibles, and the latest witticisms of "Chalaça," the palace clown.

"Domitila's influence," the Swedish ambassador with good reason reported, "is greater than it ever was before." The favorite, the truth is, was at the height of her prestige, but it was not to last for long. On the 29th, in writing to her, Dom Pedro had signed himself: "Your friend and lover until death." But on the very next day, without his being aware of it, the marchioness's fate was sealed, when Barbacena at Canterbury signed the emperor's marriage contract with the Princess Amelia Napoleon.

When the news reached Rio, Domitila had already entered upon her fourth imperial pregnancy.

By the time they reached the age of thirty-five, the marchioness had given thirteen children to the fatherland and Dom Pedro at least sixteen. May not the prince's sensuality and her extraordinary fecundity go to explain, biologically, the perfect affinity that existed between them? They were sexually suited to each other.

In April, 1831, Pedro was to abdicate the throne of Brazil and set out for Europe to reconquer the crown of Portugal for his daughter. Three years had barely passed when the marchioness gave birth to a son; before nine months more had gone by, she bore another child, and in the years that followed, four more. She had gone to live with Brigadier General Raphael Tobias, renowned political leader of São Paulo, and in seven years she gave him six heirs. It was not until June, 1842, that their union was legalized. Maria-Isabel, last offspring of the imperial couch, was then twelve years old, and she was present at the ceremony which she has ingenuously described in her own picturesque language:

We saw Mama, our family chaplain, and my *compadre* [she always called Tobias her *compadre* for the reason that she had been godmother to one of his daughters, her sister] going up toward the altar. The ceremony began, and then we saw that Mama was going to be married. When the wedding was over, Mama came up to us, kissed us, and said to me: "My daughter, I am doing this so you need never be ashamed of your mother. You are almost a young lady now, and it was necessary for me to do it." I said: "But I thought you were married to my *compadre*." It was then that I knew she had not been.

Now that the marchioness with her second marriage was leading a normal life, her temperament likewise underwent a change. Being very close to her husband, she took a lively interest in politics. At the São Paulo elections, from 1840 on, she was to be found exhibiting a fervent and militant patriotism. Breaking a lance against the conservatives, she definitely allied herself with the liberals and fought for them with an energy and devotion that were really extraordinary. One of her biographers comments:

In such a period of political effervescence, the marchioness exhibited the energy and fearlessness of the modern English suffragettes. Her resources when it came to political scheming and tactics were inexhaustible. She would put in an appearance at the polling places and firmly oppose the tricks of the opposition; and on one occasion she narrowly escaped their wrath by taking refuge at election headquarters in the parish of Our Lady of Expectation, which was a stronghold of her followers.

The same biographer relates that on a certain occasion, the conservatives having won and being desirous of staging a noisy celebration, the first thing they thought of was to obtain the services of the band in that locality. But they were too late. Anticipating her adversaries, the marchioness already had hired the band and hidden it in her house. In that way she spoiled their demonstration by depriving them of the indispensable drums and horns. In 1842, when her husband, in Sorocaba, joined the federalist revolt that had broken out in the southern part of the country, she was more than his loyal companion at all hours, she was his enthusiastic co-worker, ready for any sacrifice to bring about a rebel victory, including her own fortune, which as a matter of fact was in good part squandered in this unsuccessful political venture.

Years later, after they had been pardoned, Tobias and Domitila were to spend their declining days together in São Paulo, happily and tranquilly, surrounded by their children and looked up to by all. Always respected for his integrity, Tobias continued to represent the province in various legislatures and at one time headed the list of candidates for the Imperial Senate.

Becoming a widow for a second time in 1857, the marchioness was to survive her companion by ten years, and these last years were a true apostolate, being marked by the constant practice of virtue and Christian charity. She was frequently to be seen going along the streets and hill slopes of São Paulo with a mantilla over her head and followed by a black woman carrying a basket filled with gifts for the needy.[2] One of these latter, a poor and obscure student, had fallen victim of an epidemic of typhus. Despite the fact that she was old and in poor health herself, Domitila did not hesitate to wait on him like a nurse, and would appear at the impoverished student's lodging house to bring fruits to the patient and change his bed linen. No one would have dreamed that this youth with the keen eyes and ready answers was later to become one of the most illustrious figures in the political history of

Brazil—the Viscount of Ouro Preto, last bulwark of the monarchical order.

Domitila grew old slowly. The years appeared to be kind to her and reluctant to lay a hand upon her white skin and lovely features. In her sixties and twice a widow, one chronicler writes, she was a splendid ruin.

Time had made her unusual concessions. Age had come to her with the delicacy of one who retouches old portraits. It had gently covered her head with snow while preserving in so far as possible the haughtiness of that lovely bosom; it had breathed upon her face with a tenderness that scarcely dimmed the freshness those features once had known; it had left her sound teeth their pearly whiteness, and in her eyes there still glowed a spark in memory of the bonfires that once had been kindled there.

Once again, the shadow of Napoleon. In 1807 an attempt had been made to marry Dom Pedro to Bonaparte's niece, Murat's daughter. Years later, when the archduchesses were being allotted, Marie-Louise had been given to the emperor of the French and Leopoldina to the Brazilian prince, making him the Corsican's brother-in-law. Ten years after that, when he had become a widower, his diplomats had gone wife-hunting for him in the courts of Europe only to meet with one refusal after another from freckle-faced princesses, redheaded princesses, tall, skinny princesses, Scandinavian albinos, and buxom Germans, ladies whose hands he would have accepted by way of fulfilling the heavy obligations of a monarch with the interests of his dynasty at heart. And then, just as he had given up hope, fate had given him in place of the ugly creatures whom he had courted a bride such as he would never have dared hope for: a delightful young woman of seventeen who might have stepped out of a Reynolds or a Gainsborough painting. Such was the daughter of Eugène de Beauharnais. The smile that lighted up the oval of her face recalled her Martinique grandmother who had had at her feet the tyrant of Europe and who had worn upon her brow the imperial crown of France.

She had been born in 1812, while Napoleon was carrying on his unfortunate Russian campaign. Her father, viceroy of Italy, a man of action as well as a wise counselor, had accompanied the emperor, who did him justice when he said: "In this war we have all made mistakes; Eugène is the only one who has not." Following Bonaparte's abdication, Eugène and his wife, the Princess Amelia of Bavaria, had retired to that country where he held the title of Duke of Leuchtenberg and Prince of Eichstett. There the young Princess Amelia Napoleon had been reared, up to the time when she was discovered by agents of the Emperor of Brazil.

Dom Pedro fell in love with her the moment he saw her picture, and from then on his personal conduct was impeccable. "Chalaça" no longer recognized him. "Our master," he wrote, "ever since that picture came, has been another man; he no longer sleeps away from home but always pays his calls accompanied by chamberlains, and there is nothing new to report."

After the marriage had been celebrated in the chapel of the palace of Leuchtenberg, Amelia went by way of Ostend to Plymouth, where two Brazilian frigates were waiting for her. She embarked on August 30th in the company of her brother, Prince Auguste. Dom Pedro personally took charge of the arrangements for her reception by having them deck the city, erect arches of triumph, adorn the palaces, and hang the houses along the principal streets with bunting. His emotion at seeing the frigate *Empress,* bearing the bride whom he so desired, enter the harbor, cannot be described. Rowing vigorously, the imperial galley put out for the ship, winding its way among the hundreds of small boats that covered the bay to greet the new sovereign.

In his handsome generalissimo's uniform, the emperor eagerly climbed the gangway that was let down for him from the frigate and was conducted by the indefatigable Barbacena to meet the empress. Amelia was extremely timid at first, but she speedily recovered her self-possession and natural manner as she thanked Dom Pedro for the words of welcome which he with some difficulty had uttered in French. "Ever since that moment," writes Barbacena, "the bridal couple have been as wrapped up in each other as if they had been in love for many years, and the enthusiasm on each side is so great that at this moment I look upon them as the two happiest beings in all the world."

With senses dulled by long years of unbridled living and a heart perturbed by the cares and disillusionments of politics, Dom Pedro now felt within himself a rebirth of happiness as he gazed on this princess who had come to him like a gift from heaven. He was enchanted with Amelia's beauty, her refined manners, her soft and gentle voice, her simplicity, and above all, that irresistible smile of hers. The clouds now began to lift from the emperor's face, the lines of which had been hardened by the strain of these last years, and the roguish, jovial look was visible once more at the corners of his mouth. The whole of the stormy past had now been forgotten, as if swept away by the fresh breeze that ruffled the surface of Guanabara Bay on that springtime afternoon.

On the day following the disembarkation, the artist Louis Alexis Boulanger, acting under the instructions and supervision of the monarch himself, designed the insignia for a new order of merit which Dom Pedro had conceived: the "Order of the Rose," inspired by the little roses that, like a shower of petals, adorned the bride's gown. In the excitement attendant upon the proclamation of independence, he had instituted the Order of the Southern Cross to commemorate the founding of the empire and reward those whose had devoted themselves to the cause of Brazil; and he now paid the bride the most refined and gallant of tributes by dedicating to her this new Order which was to have as its motto the words "Love and Fidelity"—an ideal difficult of attainment for one like him, who looked upon monogamy as being not something imposed by duty and reason but rather the result of an accidental frigidity. The statesman's idea had now become the cavalier's romantic impulse; and within a short while, the wearers of the Grand Cross, the Officers and Knights of the Rose were to be displaying their impressive medals with a five-pointed star, an armillary sphere, and a delicate frame of roses in enamel and gold.

Amelia was, in truth, the person whom Pedro and Brazil needed. Devoid of the evangelical passivity and humble submissiveness that had characterized Leopoldina, she was able to exert a beneficent and wholesome influence on the court of Rio de Janeiro. The marchioness, having discreetly accepted her exile from São Cristovão, was barely a symbol, now all but effaced, of the emperor's past folly. Every trace of the favorite was promptly removed, beginning with the Duchess of Goiaz, who was packed off to school in Paris. The imperial household once more became a model Brazilian family, marked by a respect for traditions and the purity of the home. The empress did not confine herself to purely domestic affairs, such as changing everything about, altering the appearance of the palace salons, imposing an etiquette and a ceremonial on the bourgeois court and imparting to it the manners of a great lady, while overseeing everything, "even to the expenses of the pantry." She went a step further than that and played a role of some importance in the political life of Brazil. By the friendship and support she accorded the Marquis of Barbacena, she enabled him to begin with encouraging prospects of success the work of strengthening the tottering monarchy.

Gently but firmly she saw to the removal of those courtiers who were rendering the throne unpopular and who provided an easy target for the enemies of royalty.

The volcano, nevertheless, was rumbling beneath Dom Pedro's feet. The experiments in parliamentary government begun in 1827 under the leadership of the deputy Pedro de Araujo Lima, had not met with success. Barbacena's ministry, set up in December, 1829, was able to maintain itself for nearly a year, thanks to the prestige of the marquis, who effectively contributed to the clearing up, in part at least, of the deep-seated crisis; but as a result of clever intrigues, the emperor was led to break with his minister, and the latter had to abandon midway the task to which he had devoted so much ardor and patriotism. He was followed by a number of insignificant figures without the ability to advise the monarch or aid him in warding off the catastrophe which all felt was in the air. The rockbound conservative elements thereupon undertook to organize a society whose purpose should be to guard the crown against assault from anarchical factions. The "Pillars of the Throne" were to be a kind of legion charged with protecting the emperor and lending him unconditional support in defense of royalist institutions. Although Dom Pedro had repudiated the plan, which never was put into effect, it was rumored that the society was growing in numbers day by day and that its object was to proclaim him an absolute monarch like Louis XIV.

When the emperor formed his own private cabinet, headed by "Chalaça," to handle his personal correspondence, it came to be known as the "secret cabinet." In the provinces, where news arrived greatly distorted by those who spread it, this mysterious antechamber appeared surrounded by an aura of despotism; it was looked upon as hatching nefarious plans against the nation,

squandering public funds, opposing popular liberties, and merely
awaiting the opportune moment for imposing its absolute rule
upon the country. The political dramas then taking place in
France were reflected in Brazil as in a mirror, with a certain re-
fraction due to the tropics, and those three days of July, 1830,
when the Parisian mob so clamorously overturned the throne of
the absolute monarch Charles X, had a profound repercussion.
The insistent and perspicacious tongues of slanderers proceeded
to clothe with absolutist trappings Pedro's inborn liberalism, in
order that he might be pulled from the throne by the same revolutionary impulse that, starting on the French barricades, was
spreading throughout the world in the form of a fevered urge for
constitutional government.

Evaristo da Veiga, the most vigorous journalist that Brazil
ever produced, led the campaign in his paper, the *Aurora
Fluminense*. "Charles X," he declared, "has ceased to reign, and
may the same thing happen to any monarch who, betraying his
vows, shall undertake to destroy the free institutions of his
country." The assassination in São Paulo of an Italian journalist,
Libero Badaró, who had defended the French revolution of 1830
and had noisily expressed his extremist opinions, was to lead to
fresh attacks on the government, which was accused of having
inspired the crime.

Among the new personages whom Dom Pedro called upon to
help make up his cabinet was the deputy José Antônio da Silva
Maia, whose reelection by the province of Minas Gerais was indispensable to his ratification for the post. This being a point of
honor for the emperor, he decided to go in person to the provincial
capital in order to make sure of the outcome; but in those very
cities where, in 1822, he had been received with flowers and *vivas,*
the bells now in place of pealing joyously were tolling for the
death of the liberal Badaró, victim of absolutism. Upon his re-

turn to Rio, the people in the streets cried out as he passed: "Long live the emperor so long as he abides by the constitution!" Conflicts then sprang up between his adherents and the oppositionists, and there were riotous bottle-throwing nights, a harbinger of the nearing storm.

CHAPTER TWELVE

ADVENTURE BECKONS AND A CROWN
GOES BY THE BOARD

Dom Pedro was not the man to adapt himself to the routine of cabinet government, to any monotonous formula, or the disciplined mechanism of a constitutional regime. His temperament, his impulsive outbursts clashed with the proprieties of such a regime, which he looked upon as being vain and senseless. He was like those generals that win wars but do not succeed in surviving the peace. His spiritual climate was that of the epic; his pleasure lay in danger; his ambition was to achieve glory. As political difficulties piled up about him more and more in Brazil, he was increasingly attracted to the Iberian adventure. It held, indeed, an irresistible appeal for him.

He was the one who had implanted liberalism in Brazil to the scandal of all the other monarchies, but it had there been carried to unlooked-for extremes; and the exponents of the doctrine had even gone so far as to repudiate him as a renegade for not having fallen in with their excesses, their delirious Jacobinism. The revolution had outrun the one who had been its inspiration and was threatening to sweep him away in the whirlwind. But for European liberals, meanwhile, he continued to be the "Knight of Hope," and for this reason they now urged him to cross the ocean and shake the Old World with his liberating stride.

In addition to the Portuguese campaign, by means of which he dreamed of snatching from Dom Miguel the crown that belonged to his own daughter Maria da Gloria, still more grandiose plans were forming in his mind. Ever since 1826 the Spanish liberals had been urging him to return to the Peninsula in order that they might crown him king of Spain and emperor of Iberia. Ferdinand VII, the "Idolized," upon mounting the Spanish throne at the end of the year 1813, following the expulsion of the French, found that the kingdom had undergone profound changes during the five years of Napoleonic occupation. In 1812, in the midst of the struggle with France, a constitution had been adopted, free speech and a free press now prevailed, and the Inquisition was no more than a shade out of the past. Unyielding, however, in his absolutist principles, the king declared null and void the constitution and all decrees of the Cortes and proceeded to reinstate the old Council of Castile, Council of the Indies, Council of Finances, and Council of the Orders.

The stern tribunal of the Inquisition once more reopened its doors and tendered a special banquet to the king, who came to take part in its deliberations, sign the sentences that it pronounced, and visit the dark dungeons of the Holy Office. So great was the violence practiced that the former guerrillas took up arms once more in defense of those rights that the nation had won; but with the aid of scaffold and pillory, Ferdinand contrived to put down in a veritable blood bath these liberal uprisings that followed one another over a long period of years.

The successful coup was to be the one launched by the expeditionary force of the Indies, which was quartered in the suburbs of Cadiz, and had been cleverly brought about by American agents and emissaries of the liberal party. On January 1, 1820, a young officer, Don Rafael del Riego, launched the movement by a proclamation in support of the constitution. Not having succeeded in rousing Andalusia, in a burst of audacity he marched upon Estremadura with barely forty-five men. For a moment it looked as if the liberal cause were about to collapse, but this mad act on Riego's part electrified the country, and La Coruña, El Ferrol, Vigo, Saragossa, and Barcelona gave their adherence to the movement even as General Mina and his troops were entering Pampeluna. On March 7 the *Gazette* published the convocation for a new meeting of the Cortes. In Madrid the rebel mob ran through the streets shouting fiercely and went on to sack the palace of the Inquisition. It was a day that had the flavor of a Spanish 14th of July.

Ferdinand thereupon reestablished the *ayuntamiento,* swore to uphold the constitution, and summoned a temporary junta under the presidency of the archbishop of Toledo. The reversal was complete. The liberal extremists were now in command, and those who had been responsible for the pronunciamento of Cadiz were made field marshals. All had to swear loyalty to the charter, and curates received orders to explain it to their parishioners from the pulpit. In the capital, meanwhile, a couple of absolutist conspiracies had been hatched with the connivance of the king. There was great disorder in the city. Riego was greeted in the theater by the singing of the revolutionary hymn, the "Trágala." The ministers endeavored to dismiss him, but the populace rose in his favor. With no effective guarantees from the central government, the authorities in the provinces did not know which side to take, being spied upon by the absolutists on the one hand and the ultraliberals on the other, and menaced by both.

On June 30th the royal guard rose in Madrid as the Cortes ended its deliberations. General Morillo was able to restore order, but the repercussions abroad were formidable. For a week the king was practically a prisoner, his life appeared to be in danger, and the idea of intervention gained ground in the cabinets of the Holy Alliance. Incited by Czar Alexander and the French clerical party, Montmorency and Chateaubriand at the Congress of Verona proposed that an expedition be sent at once to aid Ferdinand. This plan having been approved despite the opposition of Louis XVIII and Villèle, Angoulême set out and marched across Spain from Irun to Cadiz. Madrid fell on the 19th of May. A temporary regency having been set up, its first act was to re-establish the state of things prior to 1820.

It was the Terror beginning again. Members of the "Avenging Angel" Society and royalist volunteers now started hunting down liberals, dragging them off to the pillory, tearing out their hair, and inflicting upon them every kind of torture. Prisons were attacked by infuriated mobs and the liberals held in them were massacred. It was the beginning of a reign of terror that was to last ten years. Universities were closed, academies suppressed, poets were shut up in convents, and the last remaining representatives of the municipalities were expelled. Yet even this was insufficient in the eyes of the ultraroyalists; they wanted still stronger measures and accused Ferdinand VII of weakness. It was his brother, Don Carlos, a dyed-in-the-wool absolutist, who came to be their true idol, the center of all their hopes. In the interior, meanwhile, numerous armed bands were springing up, disorder was rife, and the country was on the verge of complete anarchy.

It was at this grievous juncture that the Spanish liberals, with their fatherland transformed into a battlefield, turned their eyes toward the Emperor of Brazil, the great "Benefactor of the Peoples." He appeared to them as the one man who might be able to stop the blood-letting that was draining the energies of the nation. He was already the rightful King of Portugal; he should be the King of Spain as well and Emperor of the Peninsula. That would make him one of the most powerful sovereigns in Europe, the mainstay of liberals throughout the world. He would be the champion of the Holy Alliance of the peoples in opposition to the Holy Alliance of the kings. In a solemn memorial which they drew up and sent to Pedro, the Spaniards declared:

Your Majesty had already attracted the attention of the universe by granting independence to the Brazilian nation; but the spontaneous and generous act by which you have conferred liberty upon the Portuguese people has given Your Majesty a laurel wreath more lasting than those of all the famous princes of history. Two hemispheres repeat Your Majesty's name with enthusiasm and veneration.

After alluding to the misfortunes that had fallen upon Spain, which saw in him "its last hope," they went on to urge him to accept the "triple crown" of Brazil, Spain, and Portugal, "of which you have shown yourself so worthy." Dom Pedro was to receive the scepter in the name of "that right to the constitutional throne of our country that is recognized by the law of the land and the suffrage of all good Spaniards." The appeals made to him to come to the aid of Spain take on a pathetic quality: "May Heaven grant our heartfelt wish, and may the groans of our desolated land bring Your Majesty to us!" And Pedro is assured that "the millions of subjects upon whom Your Majesty has conferred happiness shall not love you any more than do those who now accept you as their prince!"

In 1829 the Spaniards renewed their pleas. Let Dom Pedro restore peace and prosperity to a Spain rent by civil war; his very appearance in the Peninsula would be like that of an "archangel bringing salvation." Don Alvaro Flórez Estrada, Don Francisco Díaz Morales, Don Juan Rumi, and Don Andrés Borrego were the signers of this fresh appeal. Pedro, however, was still absorbed in the task of consolidating his American empire. His work, as he saw it, was to be done one step at a time. Later he would come to Europe to transform the Peninsula into one great nation, powerful, free, and happy.

In 1830 the secret societies of Spain and Portugal held a conference, and at a joint meeting of the supreme councils a resolution of the greatest importance was adopted, to the effect that Dom Pedro was to be offered the title of "Emperor of Iberia" as preparations meanwhile were made to acclaim him as the common sovereign. A plenipotentiary by the name of Barreiros was immediately dispatched to Rio de Janeiro to transmit the terms of the offer. Already at that time the emperor was thinking of abdicating the throne of Brazil and setting out for the battle-fields of Europe. He felt that Brazil no longer wanted him but rather was anxious to have a "Brazilian" ruler in the person of his son Dom Pedro II. He even had ordered a first draft of his abdication, but noting a certain haste on the part of the minister who prepared the document, he tore it up in the councilor's face, adding a number of insults as he did so.

The one means of overcoming the Brazilian political crisis lay in forming a ministry composed of the leaders of the liberal party, but to this Dom Pedro would not agree. He would not give up the prerogative he enjoyed of choosing ministers who, above everything else, had his personal confidence; and he persisted in the obsession that he was more liberal than the liberals themselves, even as he shut them out from participation in the government. The British formula—the sovereign reigns but does not govern—was not at all suited to his domineering personality. The cautious advice that was given him to refrain from imposing his own ideas upon his ministers and to appoint to cabinet posts this or that outstanding figure in the majority party left him unmoved.

His reasoning was as inflexible as it was oversimplified. It was nothing but malicious slander when they said that he was out to do away with popular liberties; in his heart he had never harbored any designs that were not in accord with the constitution. Why then should he give up a right which that same constitution assured him, that of freely appointing or dismissing ministers according to the degree of confidence that he had in them? No, he would never do it.

On the 5th of April, 1831, irked by timid mediocrities and inept councilors around him, he dismissed his entire cabinet and appointed in its stead one made up of men who had been leaders in 1823: the Marquises of Paranaguá, Baependí, Inhambupe, and Aracaty, the Count of Lages, and the Viscount of Alcântara—making up what came to be known as the "ministry of marquises." This news aroused the greatest indignation, such an aggregation of titles being interpreted as an obvious sign of absolutist intentions on the emperor's part. Popular groups, headed by parliamentary leaders, now began gathering in the Campo de Sant'Ana and in front of the barracks, where they incited the troops to join the movement against the "marquises." The magistrates having been hastily summoned, they were charged with the task of transmitting to the emperor the will of the people, which was that he should dismiss his cabinet. Dom Pedro sent them back with a message written in his own hand. Why, he wanted to know, should they distrust the sincerity of the oath he had taken to support the constitution? Had he not given his word of honor that he would respect it? As for the ministers, they had been chosen for the reason that they were animated by similar sentiments; of that the people might rest assured.

No sooner had this message been read than it was torn to bits by the angry crowd to cries of, "Down with the ministry!"

Let the magistrates return to São Cristovão and repeat, in the name of the citizenry, the demand that those ministers dismissed the day before be reinstated.

"You may say to the people," was Dom Pedro's haughty reply, "that I have received their petition. You may further tell them that the late ministry did not merit my confidence, and that I shall do what I think best. You may remind them, also, that I am acting in accordance with the constitution. It is necessary for me to defend those rights of mine that are guaranteed by that constitution, even at the sacrifice of everything that I possess, and of my own person." And he concluded: "I am ready to do everything for the people, but nothing under compulsion by the people."

In the Campo de Sant'Ana, meanwhile, the crowd was growing every minute; and toward the end of the afternoon infantry and artillery units began drawing up alongside the demonstrators, for their officers had not been able to keep them from fraternizing with the populace. Along toward midnight the commandant at arms himself sent a message to the emperor saying that it would be sufficient to calm the minds of the rebels if His Majesty would but appoint a new cabinet composed of liberals; out of regard for his dignity, he would not be called upon to reappoint those ministers that had been dismissed. But Pedro curtly repelled the suggestion. Informed that there were still at São Cristóvão a few army units that were ready to die for him, he thanked them with deep emotion for their loyalty but added that he did not care to sacrifice them; let them, rather, go down to the Campo and join their comrades.

Major Luiz Alves de Lima, future marshal and Duke of Caxias, Brazil's greatest soldier, pleaded with him to hold out: "If Your Majesty," he said, "wishes to put down the movement, nothing could be easier. All you will have to do is to go this very night to

your Santa Cruz plantation and there assemble the militia. I myself am prepared to lead them."

"The plan," Dom Pedro answered him, "is one worthy of
the loyal Major Lima; but I cannot accept it, for I would not have
a single drop of Brazilian blood spilled for my sake. And so, let
the major and his battalion also proceed at once to the Campo
de Sant'Ana."

Major Frias, emissary of the revolutionists, was anxiously
awaiting a definitive reply as Dom Pedro strode up and down
his study, with pale face, deep-sunken eyes, and tremulous lips
that revealed the intense struggle taking place inside him. "No,"
declared the emperor finally; "it is against my honor and against
the constitution. I will abdicate first. I will die first."

The French and English ambassadors and a few intimates who
were present stood anxiously awaiting the decision. Their eyes
were upon Dom Pedro as he paced the room. At last he dropped
down into a chair and nervously dashed off a few lines. Handing
the brief message to Major Frias, he said to him in a voice shaken
with emotion: "There they have my abdication; I hope that they
will be happy. I am going to Europe, leaving behind me a country
that I have always loved and still love deeply." The French ambassador set down the emperor's words in a dispatch to the Quai
d'Orsay:

"I prefer to descend from the throne with honor rather than to
go on reigning as a sovereign who has been dishonored and de-
graded. Those born in Brazil no longer want me for the reason
that I am Portuguese. I have been expecting this for a long time,
have seen it coming ever since I visited Minas. My son has the
advantage over me in that he is a Brazilian by birth. The Brazilians
respect him. He will have no difficulty in governing, and the

constitution will guarantee him his rights. I renounce the crown with the glory of ending as I began—constitutionally."

He gave the empress a long embrace, his eyes wet with the tears he had been holding back. "He knew better how to abdicate than how to reign," wrote the French diplomat. "In the course of that unforgettable night, in the eyes of all who beheld him, the sovereign rose above himself." [1] At the first streak of dawn, amid the cries and convulsive weeping of the servants, the imperial family left the palace for the quay where the sloops of the British ship *Warspite* were waiting for them.

Peaceful and happy, unconscious of all that was going on, the crown prince Dom Pedro was quietly sleeping in the innocence of his five years. At the last moment his father came in to see him. Deeply touched, he stroked the child's fair hair and kissed him tenderly on the forehead; and then, as if making up for an omission, he also kissed the baby hand. The child was no longer his son; it was his emperor, Dom Pedro II. A few months before, Dom Pedro's most powerful enemy, José Bonifácio de Andrada, had returned from his long exile. Forgetting all the wrongs and misunderstandings of the past, the emperor in the last act that he signed appointed José Bonifácio as tutor and guardian of his four children. At that moment he made no distinction between friends and enemies but recognized in the rebel of yesterday the most upright, honorable, and sincere person that he knew, and accordingly confided to him all he had that was most precious. The courtiers made horrified eyes at this, but Dom Pedro showed that he knew human nature better than they did. This gesture on his part profoundly moved the aged Andrada, who from that moment on became the most fervid and loyal of supporters.

The abdication marked an end, but it also heralded a new be-

ginning, a new dawn. Before him Dom Pedro had not only the
military reconquest of Portugal and the restoration of the throne
to his daughter Maria da Gloria, but he further had, to lead him
on, the dream of setting up once more the ancient Hispanic Empire as envisaged by Philip II, that "Fifth Empire" of those Portuguese myths centering about King Sebastian. Brazil has been an
episode in his life, certainly the most impressive one thus far;
but new ones now awaited him upon the battlefields of Europe,
the most arduous and the noblest of them all.

He had lived surrounded by crowns; but on that early April
morning in 1831, he was merely the Duke of Braganza, the subject of his own son Dom Pedro II, Emperor of Brazil, and of his
daughter, the little Princess Maria da Gloria, Queen of Portugal.

Before beginning the armed struggle against his brother
Miguel, Dom Pedro was once more to measure his strength with
Metternich in the arena of European politics. The question of
John VI's successor was an aspect of the life-and-death struggle
that was taking place throughout Europe between liberalism and
absolutism, and this clash of principles was at once to relegate
to a secondary plane the individual rights of the two principal
claimants to the Portuguese throne. At the moment the thing that
mattered was the political complexion of the aspirants. Once that
had been resolved, capable jurists would see to making the law
fit the pretensions of one or the other.

Dom Pedro had been commonly accepted as the legitimate
heir by all the courts of Europe, up to the moment when it became known that he "of his own free will" had granted the Portuguese a constitution. Some weeks before, Metternich himself had
explained the matter to a foreign diplomat. "Portugal," he had
said, "is not the empire of the Incas, where younger brothers succeed the older ones to the prejudice of the latter's children. Dom

Pedro has a daughter, and Dom Miguel consequently has no claim whatever to put forward." It was not until after news had come of the granting of the charter that the first allegations in favor of Dom Miguel began to be made.

Metternich, who pulled the strings in all the chancelleries of Europe, then resolved to settle the Portuguese question in his own way. Dom Miguel was his trump card. He had reared the prince under his own supervision and counted upon making of him a docile but powerful instrument. Once he was in Lisbon, at the head of the regency, Miguel would annul that crazy charter of Dom Pedro's and would stamp out radicalism in the Peninsula once and for all. The second point of his plan consisted in luring the little queen to Vienna under pretext of completing her education alongside her grandfather. As the child's warden, he would be able to impose his solution on Dom Pedro by forcing the latter to make the best of the *coup d'état* that Miguel was to stage. However, the haste with which Miguel's followers in Lisbon acclaimed the prince as their king, without that circumspection which Metternich had advised, led to the frustration of this second stage in the chancellor's scheme. Yielding to the insistence of his father-in-law, the Emperor of Austria, Pedro had sent his daughter to Europe in the charge of the Marquis of Barbacena; but the latter, touching at Gibraltar on his way to Vienna, got wind of the latest events in Portugal and at once changed his itinerary by having the Brazilian frigate on which they were traveling put in at Falmouth.

Metternich's disappointment was boundless. He at once sent the Count von Lebzeltern to England with instructions to bring the princess back at any cost, and he further instructed his diplomats in London to use any arguments with the Brazilian representatives that might attain their end—"anything from flattery to threats." But Barbacena, who had smelled out the chancellor's intentions from afar, proved impossible to handle. Metternich even resorted to bribery and offered anything and everything, money, honors, no matter what. Let him but bring Maria da Gloria to Vienna and he might fix his own reward, honorary titles and *pecuniary gratification,* "no matter how high it might come." [2]

Although the European powers in view of Miguel's flagrant act of usurpation had withdrawn their representatives from Lisbon, they were secretly exultant over the suppression of the charter and were merely waiting for a pretext to reestablish diplomatic relations with the absolute monarch. This was true even of England, which, now that Canning was no more—his death had been described by De Gentz, Metternich's lieutenant, as "a blessing from on high"—was dominated by the Wellington-Aberdeen combination. The landing of Maria II at Falmouth greatly embarrassed the English government. There was nothing for it, however, but to accord her the honors due a sovereign, and so the Iron Duke at once began putting forth his best efforts to rid himself of these inconvenient guests. After having advised Barbacena to take her to Vienna or else back to Brazil, since England could not give her any help, he had the rudeness to tell him quite frankly that, "even supposing the queen had the right on her side, the Portuguese did not want any other ruler than Dom Miguel." [3]

There was but one obstacle to Miguel's recognition by England, and that was that he represented the ultranationalist tendency that was profoundly hostile to the centuries-old British guardianship and that favored, rather, a close collaboration with France and Spain. From Lisbon the British representative Lamb advised the cabinet in London that the Miguel government "releases the country from its ancient dependence upon us." Herein lay the key to British vacillations: commercial interests in the island feared the formation of a Portuguese nationalist state that would deprive them of their import monopoly. But Wellington, nevertheless—his ultra-Tory cabinet was about to fall—ended by deciding for Miguel. By what seemed an act of providence for Dom Pedro, the ship bearing the formal recognition to Portugal was overtaken by a violent storm and had to return to Plymouth. In the meanwhile, Wellington had left the government, and his successor, Grey, held up the voyage.

Spain, Russia, the Vatican, and the United States of America all recognized Miguel. France, under the leadership of Polignac, and Austria were preparing to follow suit when there suddenly broke out in Paris the revolution that brought down the throne of Charles X and brought in the liberal-bourgeois monarchy of Louis Philippe. By its world-wide repercussions this event hastened Dom Pedro's downfall in Brazil but at the same time opened for him the most favorable perspectives in Europe. England was now passing from the obscurantism of Wellington to the intrepid liberalism of Palmerston. Paraphrasing in reverse the motto of the Holy Alliance, the Foreign Office announced that its new policy was "to support constitutional monarchies everywhere against despotic ones." Thanks to this favorable state of mind, not only in England but in France as well, Pedro was received with open arms in both capitals, being deliriously acclaimed in the streets as "the most legitimate champion of liberty."

In the England of the Whigs, the ex-emperor of Brazil was able without concealment to begin recruiting soldiers for his Portuguese expedition. Louis Philippe for his part, impelled by public opinion, placed at the disposition of the Portuguese emigrees, the ports of Quiberon, Isle de Re, and Belle Isle for the concentration and equipment of the fleet and the embarkation of troops. The struggle between Pedro and Miguel was to arouse the passions of the entire world just as in our day the Spanish civil war has done, and Portugal was to be transformed into a battlefield where the two ideologies were to fight it out. Regimes and individuals were to intervene, directly or indirectly, staking their fate upon the final outcome of the conflict. Among them, on the one hand, were liberals from every land, former officers of the Brazilian army, Napoleonic veterans with their showy insignia, and many others; all came running to enlist at the recruiting offices which Dom Pedro had opened in London and Paris. Dom Miguel's army on the other hand was joined by the legitimists, chiefly French, including a number of outstanding generals: Bourmont, Clouet, Almer, La Rochejacquelein, Tannegui-Duchâtel, and Grival, veterans of the Vendée.

Over one island, and one only, in the Azores, the Third Island, the banner of Maria II still waved. That island had held out obstinately against all the attacks of Miguel's fleet, with an in-explicable loyalty in which destiny seemed to have a hand. And it was from this eagle's nest in mid-ocean that Dom Pedro and his liberals were to launch forth upon the great adventure. Amelia, in the meantime, was about to give birth, and Pedro was as much absorbed with the expectation of this event as he was with prepara-tions for the imminent struggle. His thoughts went back and forth between the arsenals and camps and the palace of Meudon, whose historic salons, decorated in the most refined taste, had provided a home for the former Empress of Brazil. He was un-willing to leave before he had held in his arms the fruit of his great love for Amelia of Leuchtenberg; and accordingly, the expedition was postponed, battle plans were altered, and Miguel, with eighty thousand men in readiness, was kept waiting as all Europe watched for the campaign to start; but because of an unborn child, the impatience of the troops and the eagerness of a fleet ready to give battle had to be held in check by a delicate bit of sentiment.

On December 1 the little one was born. It was a girl, and Dom Pedro named her Amelia. She was solemnly baptized with French royalty as her sponsors. "Although she was born in Paris," her father declared, "she is Brazilian, seeing that she was conceived before my abdication." Dom Pedro did not wish to abandon his wife nor the infant by whose cradle he stood. At times he seemed to have forgotten all the rest of the world, the campaign about to be launched, the call of glory and adventure. It was Amelia who encouraged him, brought him back to reality, by urging him to control his heart and unsheath the liberating sword. Spartan resignation lay behind this sensible advice of hers which finally awakened the Braganza from his slumber and a dream that could not be.

CHAPTER THIRTEEN

ON THE BATTLEFIELDS OF PORTUGAL

The tranquil little port of Belle Isle at the beginning of the year 1832 presented a wholly unwonted aspect. It had been chosen as the point of concentration for the Portuguese emigrees and those volunteers who had enlisted for the civil war that was soon to break out in the Peninsula. The hubbub in the streets and the babel of tongues astonished the good people of Brittany; primitive and peaceful by nature, they did not know what to make of this influx of foreigners. On the 2nd of February the Duke of Braganza arrived. Leaving Paris on the 25th of January, he had traveled by carriage to Nantes, where he had taken a steamer for the island. On the eve of his departure he had been at the Tuilleries, where Louis Philippe had warmly wished him success in the expedition he was undertaking. His farewell to his daughter was touching in the extreme. With deep emotion, Dom Pedro had kissed her hand, saying: "My lady, here stands a Portuguese general who goes to defend your rights and restore to you your crown." Maria da Gloria wept and fell in his arms, and her father, pressing her to his bosom, gave her a long and tender embrace.

The emperor stayed but a few days at Belle Isle. On the 10th he sailed for the Azores on the frigate *Queen of Portugal*. He was accompanied by Palmela, Cândido José Xavier, the Marquis of Loule, Padre Marcos Preto, his confessor; Mouzino da Silveira, Paulo Martins de Almeida, Captain Bastos, the Count of Saint-Leger, and a M. de Lasteyrie, Lafayette's grandson. Sartorius, a former officer of the British navy, was in command of the fleet, the other vessels including the frigate *Dona Maria II,* the brig *Third Island,* and a few transports. The corvette *Amelia* remained at Belle Isle to serve as a convoy, a few days later, to four ship-loads of volunteers.

Not a single detail of the expedition was to escape Dom Pedro's attention. On the way he composed an anthem as spontaneous and beautiful as the one he had improvised for Brazilian independence ten years before:

> For Queen and Charter is our flag unfurled
> That on the ocean breeze doth proudly wave,
> Our cause is noble, honor leads us on
> To right a grievous wrong and freedom save.

Third Island, where Dom Pedro disembarked amid enthusiastic cheers, was an armed camp swarming with people of every description: liberals out of the 1820's, fanatic and demagogic in spirit; young graduates and students fresh from the benches of the University of Coimbra, full of theories and idealism; writers and poets still given to literary fantasies; veterans of the Peninsular Campaign, admirable relics of the old Portuguese army; volunteers from every corner of Europe, ready for anything that would serve the cause of liberty; inflexible legitimists, who saw in Maria da Gloria the symbol of dynastic succession; and dreamers and adventurers who had been recruited in the streets of London and Paris and incorporated into the warrior host of the Most Faithful Queen. From then on Dom Pedro did not have a moment's rest. "He lent a hand to the mechanics in the arsenals, superintended the calking of ships in the dock, watched

them mount the artillery, and scrawled dispatches on his knee."
The English admiral Napier confessed that he had never seen a
more active human being.

At night he still found time to keep up his correspondence.
To the Marquis of Cantagalo in Brazil he described the difficulties
of the expedition, and concluded:

It is in this manner that the worthy show themselves to be true
liberals and not by words and high sounding talk; unfortunately
we have some of the latter kind in Brazil. I hope this month or by
the middle of next to head an expedition that will overthrow
tyranny and afford unequivocal proof of my disinterestedness
and of my love for the cause of Liberty properly understood.

To Dom Pedro II he offered advice worthy of Marcus
Aurelius—the "last ignoramus of the family" had not ceased to
concern himself with the education of his children. He wrote:

The time when princes were respected simply because they
were princes is past. In the century in which we are living, with
the peoples fully informed as to their rights, it is necessary that
princes should be equally well informed and realize that they are
men and not divinities; it is indispensable that they should have
broad knowledge and the good opinion of their subjects in order
that they may be loved even more than they are respected—the
respect of a free people for their ruler should spring from the
conviction that he is the leader capable of enabling them to attain
that degree of well-being to which they aspire; if this is not the
case, then it is unhappy leader, unhappy people!

The Don Juan in Pedro had not been wholly extinguished as
yet, and the beauty of the women of the Azores did not go un-
perceived by him. Despite his exhausting tasks by day and his
tender memories of Meudon, on many nights he would muffle

himself up in his ample cloak and go out in search of a pair of pretty eyes. In Angra he was to leave behind him a royal bastard to mark his passage.

On the 6th of June there was a general review. On the sea the white sails of fifty ships were lined up. They were troop transports and warships. On the island, drawn up in rows, 7,500 bayonets flashed in the sun. As Dom Pedro approached, the cannons roared and belched fire, the drums beat noisily until the earth trembled, and the trumpets blared in a merry burst of sound. There were frantic cheers as handkerchiefs waved in the air and thousands of voices shouted *vivas* and joined in the singing of martial songs. They sang the "Hymn of the Charter" which he had composed, they sang "Rule Britannia" and the "Marseillaise," hymn of all the world. On that radiant day there was not merely hope, there was the absolute certainty that victory was theirs.

On the morning of the 23rd, Mass was said in the fields at Relvão, and on the 27th the fleet put out from Ponta-Delgada and turned its prows toward the fatherland. The transports were escorted by Sartorius's ships. There were two frigates, the flagship *Queen of Portugal* with fifty-six guns, and the *Dona Maria II* with forty-eight, the brigs *Vila Flor* and *Liberal*, eight schooners, the corvette *Amelia,* and the barge *Regency,* in addition to eighteen flat-bottom lighters, their hulls armored with wooden plates and with a platform mounting a short six-caliber cannon.

Learning through his agents that Dom Miguel had concentrated the bulk of his forces, consisting of 25,000 infantrymen and 2,000 cavalrymen in the suburbs of Lisbon and that in the course of three or four days he would be able to assemble more than 40,000 men for the defense of that city, Dom Pedro decided to effect a landing in the vicinity of Oporto. This was the most vulnerable point along the seacoast, being garrisoned only by the fourth army division under the command of Santa Marta. The second city of the realm, Oporto appeared to offer every advantage. With enormous stores of foodstuffs of every sort and a population that was traditionally liberal, it might be quickly transformed into a powerful base of operations once the ranks of the invaders had been further increased by those who were certain to join the movement.

On April 7th they sighted land. For long days, though they had kept an anxious watch, they had not glimpsed a single enemy sail. Fortune must be protecting them; but still they found it hard to understand why the Miguelist fleet, which was in every way superior, had not met them in a frontal attack with the object of dispersing the convoy, sinking the ships, and routing the expedition. The aeromechanical signal system, however, which was located in Vilar south of the river Douro, had already announced that Dom Pedro's vessels were heading for a point north of Oporto, and at nine o'clock at night the drums had begun beating to put the city on the alert. There was a general tumult, and Santa Marta quickly dispatched the brigade commanded by José Cardoso de Meneses to Vila-do-Conde, and he himself with the rest of the troops set out for the Lavre Beach. Dom Pedro all the while continued sailing along the coast until he came to Vila-do-Conde, where he sent word to General Cardoso demanding that the latter join the army of liberation. Not being able to sway the Portuguese commander, he had the fleet put in and cast anchor at a distance of less than a rifle shot from Arnosa-de-Pampelido Beach.

It was indeed a bold move, his landing at this point, between two enemy forces that might by a rapid encircling movement have crushed the small expedition by hemming it in between two lines of fire. The constitutionalist troops took up a position on the beach and nervously awaited the attack, but not a shot was heard. Shortly afterward the legendary Fifth Battalion cautiously

advanced as far as Pedras-Rubras, the marine battalion occupied
Perafita, and Schwalbach, one of Dom Pedro's best captains, led
the Second and Third Chasseurs to the little chain of hills that
runs to Leça-da-Palmeira. The road was open in all directions. The
soldiers eyed one another uncomprehendingly, and the generals
exchanged questioning glances.

Santa Marta rapidly fell back to Oporto, crossed the city and,
silently and mysteriously, took up a new position on the heights
of Vila-Nova. Close on his heels came the Second and Third
Chasseurs, who entered the city by the Leça road early on the
morning of July 9th. Some hours later, mounted on a young
charger, Dom Pedro arrived with the remainder of the troops.
The rua de Cedofeita, down which the liberators marched with
hydrangeas stuck in their elevated rifle barrels, was strewn with
flowers; the ladies, clad in blue and white, the Queen's colors,
crowded the gaily bedecked windows of the praça Nova, while
the men, with blue emblems in their hats, came running up from
all sides to give the Duke of Braganza a fitting ovation.

The liberals were soon to be bitterly deceived. The four hundred men who had been sent to take over Braga and Guimarães
had met with a cold reception there and shortly afterward were
chased by large Miguelist forces. The hoped-for desertions from
the other side were inexplicably slow in coming. The entire realm
appeared to be preserving a hostile silence.

It was then that Dom Pedro had a partial glimpse of the cruel
reality of things. As someone was to put it: "Oporto was a cage;
he had fallen into a trap!" This was indeed the truth. Little by
little he came to perceive why it was that the powerful Miguelist
fleet had not come out to disperse the expedition on the high
seas; why it had abandoned the second city of the realm without
firing a shot; why it was that the royalist generals had retired at
the very moment when they had the liberals between two lines

of fire and might easily have wiped them out. The pieces were beginning to fit together, the facts becoming clear.

The fortresses of Foz and Queijo, as well as others, had been completely abandoned, and Foz was a magnificent one; provided with good powder mines, rockets, and other incendiary devices, it might have inflicted a terrible punishment upon the ships of the invaders; and properly stocked with provisions and furnished with cannon, it would have been able to hold out against all the attacks of the expeditionaries until sufficient reinforcements had been brought up to drive off the assailants. The coincidences kept piling up, pointing to a hidden hand that was tracing the inexorable course of events. Crossing the Douro on his retreat, Santa Marta had "forgotten" to put out of commission a very large number of small boats in which the liberals might cross to the other bank and continue the pursuit. He had left the boats there as an invitation to penetrate ever deeper into Portuguese territory.

Palmela, dumfounded by it all, wrote in his autobiographical notes that the Miguelist generals had certainly "lost their heads." But he was wrong. The royalist leaders were merely putting into execution a dark plan that would enable them to surround the liberal forces in the interior of the country and there exterminate them, "so that not a one would escape." In that way Dom Pedro's party would be destroyed forever. A Brazilian general, who was in Oporto when Pedro arrived, tells us in his *Memoirs* that the city had been handed over to the liberals "in pursuance of secret instructions." According to him, this was done in order to give the government "an opportunity to crush the city with fire bombs and grenades, cannon balls, and incendiary missiles . . . to see if as a result of the bombs the inhabitants of Oporto would not abandon their constitutionalist proclivities."

The Miguelist commander himself, the Viscount of Santa

Marta, in a jubilant letter to a friend, stated: "What I told you is certainly going to happen; they are certainly going to die by cannon ball or hunger or be burned alive and the worthy city of Oporto with them." An official Portuguese publication asserts that "on the very day that Dom Pedro's fleet put out from Ponta-Delgada the government at Lisbon was informed by the Portuguese consul in London of the number of warships and transports in the fleet, their respective names, of the incapacity of the so-called warships and their lack of artillery and ammunition, and the number of soldiers as well as the names of the commanding officers and the rank they held." The writer goes on to say that this same consul had recommended that a good frigate, well armed and equipped, be sent out to meet the expedition, as he judged this would be sufficient to disperse it; and the article concludes: "The government brushed aside this advice on the part of its zealous and enthusiastic servant, and *ordered that the troops be freely permitted to land in order that they might be encircled and cut to pieces as soon as they had left the seacoast and had proceeded a certain distance inland.*"

In the minds of the Miguelist generals, Dona Carlota Joaquina's fierce admonition was ringing still: "Cut off heads for me! Cut off heads for me! The French Revolution cut off forty thousand, and the population did not diminish for all of that." But Dom Pedro was not the man to be intimidated. His great moments were his tragic moments, and he knew how to face them with a bravura that was truly theatrical. He now sent the transports away, thus, like Hernán Cortez, the conqueror of Mexico, depriving the fainthearted of the hope of fleeing by sea. The situation was definitely unfavorable. To think of marching on Lisbon was out of the question, for he did not have a single squadron of cavalry and his artillery was not such as to permit of large-scale operations. On the other hand, to rest solely upon the defensive would be a flagrant admission of discouragement. The people of the kingdom on whom he had counted so blindly still remained silent and indifferent. It mattered little what were the causes of this apathy, whether a sincere loyalty to Dom Miguel, a fanaticism inspired by the friars against the Freemasons, or a fear of man-hunting reprisals on the part of Miguel's followers. The one thing that was certain was that absolutist reinforcements were bearing down upon Oporto from every corner of the country while the liberals continued to entrench themselves in their positions.

Aware of the dangers of inaction, Pedro sent out a column to reconnoiter in Valongo on July 22nd. It bore down upon the cavalry which was defending the place and succeeded in routing the enemy; but as the enthusiastic liberals were giving pursuit, they found themselves surrounded by greatly superior forces. They stood their ground bravely but were finally obliged to fall back with heavy losses to Rio-Tinto, halfway along the road to Oporto. To have attempted to bring in the remnants of the vanquished column would have been to precipitate a final rout. The thing that must be done was to reunite all the troops and strike a decisive blow at once, one that would produce a resounding victory; for anything less than a complete victory would have meant the end of everything.

On the night of the 22nd, Dom Pedro girded on his sword and, leaving only two or three hundred men in Oporto, set out at the head of what was left of his army, in the direction of Rio-Tinto, where he encountered the survivors of Valongo. Having divided his forces into three columns, he began the march upon the enemy. The right wing followed the São Cosme road; the center followed the Valongo highway; while the left, under Colonel Hodges, circled around to fall upon the Miguelists' right.

At eleven o'clock on the morning of the 23rd, the columns

marched out on the field of battle. As soon as the enemy's outposts had been dispersed, they found themselves confronting
Santa Marta's three divisions stationed on the Ponte-Ferreira
River with their rearguard resting on the hill of the same name.
There were 12,000 men in all, 200 horses, and 5 pieces of artillery.
While Schwalbach's light brigade, heading the center column,
sustained the enemy's fire, the French battalion and Shaw's rifle-
men forded the river and valiantly attacked the Miguelists' right,
breaking it up at the point of their bayonets. Santa Marta then
began moving up large reinforcements from his left wing to
succor the right, which had been almost wiped out.

At this juncture, if the commander of the liberals' right wing
had swiftly advanced upon the enemy's left, which had been
greatly weakened, the victory would have been complete; but
he did nothing of the sort, and this mistake permitted Santa
Marta to recover his lost positions by decimating the French
battalion commanded by Major Chichiri, a Tatar, who fell fighting bravely. The battle raged on. With reinforcements sent him
by the count of Vila-Flor, to whom Dom Pedro had confided the
high command, Hodges by a heroic effort succeeded in occupying once more those positions that Santa Marta had retaken
on his right, even as the center column was marching upon the
royalists and dislodging them. It was only then that Dom Pedro's
right, with its ranks undepleted, came charging into action. So
violent was the attack that the Miguelist general was compelled
to scale the mountain at his rear and beat a retreat just as night
was falling, along the Baltar highway, in the greatest disorder and
with his last cartridge gone.

Having won the great battle, Dom Pedro might have pursued
the enemy and routed what was left of the royalist army, driving
it out of the province of Minho, across the Tamega and Vouga
rivers. Then, indeed, it would have been possible to have begun

the dreamed-of march on Lisbon. At that moment, however, a wholly unexpected event occurred, one that is still enveloped in mystery, and within a few hours it had changed the aspect of things, preventing Pedro from reaping all the advantages won by his triumph.

It was three o'clock in the morning, on the 24th. The city of Oporto was holding a victory celebration. The houses were full of lights and church bells were pealing joyfully. The people were marching through the streets shouting *vivas* to the charter and to Dom Pedro. And at that point the military governor received the false news that the Viscount of Santa Marta had surprised and counterattacked the liberals bivouacked on the field and had annihilated them completely. The Duke of Braganza was reported to have already gone aboard ship at Matozinhos, while the Miguelists were said to have crossed the Douro and to be bearing down on Oporto. Believing this information to be true, the governor assembled all the troops that remained in the city, packed up all the public documents and had them put in boats and towed outside the harbor by a steamer, and himself prepared to depart.

Word of this spread throughout the city in a few minutes' time and produced an unheard-of panic. Municipal authorities, ministers of state, the superintendent of police, judges, soldiers, all fought for a place on the *Borodino,* for they all remembered the scenes that had occurred in 1828, the scaffolds, the horrible reprisals of the Miguelists. Women with bundles of clothing under their arms ran terrified through the streets, uttering cries of desperation. Upon hearing of these events, which might have the gravest consequences, Dom Pedro hastened to Oporto to calm the inhabitants. Assuming command of the army in person, he appointed as a new governor of the city a major of engineers, Bernardo de Sá Nogueira, at the same time dispatching Palmela to England in search of money and soldiers. He was disillusioned with the offensive operations outside Oporto; the people of the realm remained deaf to his appeals, and Dom Miguel's ranks were being swollen every day with fresh recruits. The only thing to do was shut himself up in Oporto, fortify the city, and hold out. Such was the aspect that the war had taken on.

At the beginning of August, the liberals made a few more sallies, one at Grijo which was successful, and one at Souto-Redondo which proved disastrous. What helped Dom Pedro more than anything else was the rivalry that existed between the two royalist generals. If Póvoas, stationed on the south bank of the Douro, upon hearing the cannon of Ponte-Ferreira, had come to the aid of his comrade when the battle was still undecided, the liberals would have been completely routed; but he preferred to remain impassive rather than contribute to his rival's success in crushing the adversary. It did not even occur to him, apparently, to threaten Oporto, which had been left without a garrison, or to capture some of the key positions of the city such as Mount Pilar.

By early September, thanks to Dom Pedro's prodigious activity and Sá Nogueira's tireless energy, the first line of defense had already been mapped out, with ten batteries commanding the highways leading to the city. This line began at Quinta-da-China, ran north by way of Campanhã and Bonfim, where it turned west by way of Povoa-de-Cima and Carvalhido, extending southward to the Bicalho Quay, where it ended. Around each of the batteries parapets were constructed and broad, deep trenches were dug, constituting the so-called "redoubts with a neck." Inside these were then installed what were known as "compression globes," that is to say, mines charged with a large quantity of powder that would explode when the enemy penetrated the fortifications. There was a second line of defenses in addition to these external ones, consisting of crossbeams, felled trees, and entrench-ments, together with mines and powder trains; these served to fortify the entrances to the long streets that ran through the center of the town and the communicating cross streets.

It was harsh experience that was to reveal the faults of this system. The two vital points, for example, Foz and Mount Pilar, had not received the necessary attention. Soult, in 1809, had not been able to maintain his position in Oporto simply because he had failed to fortify the hill, and the same was true of Foz—the mouth of the Douro—since it signified communication with the outside world, with the sources of men and armaments, and the markets for foodstuffs of every kind that, one way or another, sustained the city until the siege was lifted. Peso-da-Régua, however, who in order to eliminate the rivalry between Póvoas and Santa Marta, had assumed command of the royalist army, perceived nothing of this; the fate of the town was in his hands, but he did not so much as suspect it. Keeping watch on the liberals from afar, he remained quiet, without knowing how or when to attack.

It was not until the 22nd of July that he began large-scale troop movements, which led to the belief that a general attack was to be launched against the Oporto lines. Dom Pedro thereupon went to the batteries in order to take personal command of the artillery. Powder trains were now prepared, mines were loaded and set up in the streets, and redoubts and batteries were manned as the liberal troops stood at their posts and awaited the beginning of the action. Hours went by and no attack came. It had been no more than a reconnaissance. There were days and weeks, a month and a half, of tense waiting.

On September 10th the systematic bombardment of the city began, marked by the use of asphyxiating gases; for some of the bombs "contained blankets saturated with sulphur and soaked in a solution that gave off dense fumes and suffocating vapors that were unendurable." It was another mistake on the part of the royalists, seeing that it only inured the raw recruits from the city and, for that matter, the people as a whole to the hardships of war until they came to look upon the gravest perils with a surprising degree of indifference. However intense the cannonading was, there were always men and women to be seen at the most dangerous points, watching the attacks and sacrificing their lives with the utmost daring and foolhardiness. The lads in the street could tell from the hissing and detonation of the enemy's bombs the kind of projectiles that were being used and would throw themselves on the ground while the bombs were exploding and then would run up and examine the fragments. On the other hand, so far as the royalists were concerned, these bombardments were not only costly affairs (each mortar shot representing for Dom Miguel an outlay of nine and a half escudos),* they also considerably weakened the fighting morale of the besiegers by accustoming them to the passive calm of their encampments. From this point of view, it would have been better for them to have taken the field in a full-scale attack.

Peso-da-Régua still did not feel sufficiently strong to take the city by assault; but so great was the impatience of the Lisbon government that he found himself obliged to hasten the course of events, and a general attack was accordingly scheduled for the 29th of September, St. Michael's Day. Two days before that date a proclamation was read to the troops, conveying the assurance that the constitutionalists would very shortly be dislodged from the city of Oporto, "their last, futile refuge." There was not a Miguelist in all the land who doubted for a moment that the assault would be successful. At last the time had come to chastise the heretics, those infamous ones, the enemies of God and of religion; the land was to be cleansed of Freemasonry. Oporto

* Approximately $25, a considerable amount at that time.

was not merely a center of rebellion; it was also a cage. "Not a single one shall escape."

There were Te Deums in all the cities.

At Ajuda the sacred Host was exposed and Dom Miguel spent the day in prayer. In Braga the churches were lighted up, and there were special services for a victory that was beyond a doubt. At the Church of the Angels in Lisbon, the rabid Friar Fortunato preached to the pious congregation that had gathered to hear him, and in an outburst of frenzy, the effect either of his own rhetoric or of a feverish hallucination, he cried out: "Victory, my dearest brethren, victory! We are entering Oporto! *Te Deum laudamus!*" The women beat their foreheads in accordance with the rite and a long canticle was sung in unison as an action of grace to Almighty God.

St. Michael's Day dawned gloomy and overcast. Enveloped in mist, two enemy columns of five thousand men each marched against the city from the east. The first column, despite the heavy fire from the batteries, kept on to Campanha, forced the defenders' lines, and made its way into the city as far as the former rua do Prado, today the Street of Heroes, where it was repelled at the point of the bayonet by the French under the Count of Saint-Leger. The second column swept before it the marine battalion, decimating it to such an extent that there were barely two noncommissioned officers left to command the force. Approximately five thousand Miguelists charged the Cativo battery and succeeded in making their way up to the parapet and entrance of Praça-das-Flores. In front of Monte-Pedral, another detachment took the Medalhas redoubt, defended by an outpost of the first battalion of the third infantry; but it was dislodged shortly afterward by Captain Moniz and thirty men. Occupying the Lomba battery, the Miguelists put it out of commission by spiking all the guns. Carvalhido and Covelo were likewise strongly attacked, and Mount Pilar had to hold out against the combined attack of three columns vigorously supported by artillery.

Finally, after eleven hours of stubborn and bloody fighting, the royalists fell back to their positions, leaving more than four thousand of their number on the field of battle. Oporto now came to look upon itself as invincible, while the besiegers were convinced of their own weakness. They returned to the charge on the 14th of October, hurling five thousand men against Mount Pilar and again retreating, with 1,500 losses. It was no use. Only by an absolute blockade, by choking off all the sources of supplies, would they be able to compel the city to surrender.

To Santa Marta fell the task of applying the new system of warfare. Assuming command on the 4th of November, he notified the British government of his intention of cutting off the mouth of the Douro by means of powerful batteries. This he did; and from December 7th to the end of the war no ship succeeded in entering the river. Only a narrow neck of land, running from Foz until a little beyond the Luz lighthouse, connected the city with the rest of the world. With the situation growing more critical each day, Pedro resolved to seek the collaboration of two experienced generals, the Frenchman Solignac and the Portuguese Saldanha.

Saldanha was one of the most extraordinary soldiers of his age. A captain at seventeen, a major at nineteen, and a lieutenant colonel at twenty-two, he had commanded an operational division against the French when he was twenty-three and had won thirteen medals for bravery. When the Peninsular Campaign ended in 1814, he had been sent to Montevideo, where with boldness and decision he had faced the fierce gauchos of the pampas. By the time Brazil achieved its independence, he was captain general of the province of Rio Grande. Having been

sent as a prisoner to Rio de Janeiro for not having joined the
movement, he had been freed at once by Dom Pedro, who had
offered him the title of marquis, whatever land allotments he
might wish, the post of major general of the army, and other
honors in case he should agree to remain in the country; but
Saldanha had refused everything, having some months before
sent word to his sovereign: "I shall never fail in those duties that
honor and loyalty demand of me." He then had left for Portugal
with a little more than twenty-five escudos to his name.* When
in 1826 Pedro had granted the Portuguese a charter, the regency,
under the intimidating pressure of the Spanish ambassador, had
opposed its publication. Perceiving the danger to the new institutions that was involved in such a maneuver, Saldanha had sent
the government an ultimatum: either the charter would be sworn
to immediately or he would have the army see that it was. Forced
to emigrate the following year by the Miguelist tide that swept
over the country, he had been waiting in exile for an opportunity
to return to his native land.

Difficulties of an international nature had prevented his taking
part in the expedition of liberation. The Spanish government
had promised Pedro that it would remain neutral in the civil war
so long as Saldanha did not take part; if he did, then Spain would
place at Miguel's disposition an army of forty thousand men.
Such was the fear inspired in Ferdinand II by those plans of
Iberian unification that Saldanha had conceived in the course of
his victorious campaigns across the Peninsula. Upon arriving at
Oporto, he saw at a glance the gravity of the situation. The city's
breath of life depended upon that strip of land at Foz where munitions of war and rations were brought in to sustain its defenders.
Once this road to the sea was cut off, capitulation would be a
matter of days. It was essential that not a minute be lost, for the

* Approximately $60, at the present rate.

enemy appeared to realize at last that the outcome of the war depended upon the possession of that vital point and was accordingly preparing to take it. Having fortified Castro, the Miguelists sent out a strong column which, dislodging the liberals from the Pinhal hillock, brought within range of their guns the little stretch of beach by which Oporto maintained its communications.

In the course of seventeen days of feverish activity and insuperable daring, Saldanha succeeded in setting up two new batteries whose cross fire neutralized the effect of the important Miguelist redoubts that were threatening the Foz highway. Taking the enemy by surprise, he led his sappers to a distance of less than half a rifle shot from the adversaries' position. Transforming into a rampart the empty hogs heads that he found all over the city, he had trenches dug in front while at the rear, with the rapidity of lightning, he threw up breastworks under a lively fire from the royalist advance guard, which made a number of sallies. Between the batteries he stationed numerous artillery posts at those precise points that would afford the advantage of a converging cross fire.

On the morning of March 4th, the enemy advanced with ten thousand men to raze these new fortifications which had not yet been finished, but was repelled with more than one thousand losses. He returned to the charge on the 24th. Another disaster for him and considerable losses. The road to the sea had been saved.

Yes, the road to the sea had been saved; but nature was to succeed where the Miguelists had failed. From February on, the coast was lashed with stiff gales from the southeast accompanied by the hardships of a severe winter that brought tremendous rains and dense fogs to the city. The sea ran so high that no boat could put in, and for thirty or forty days, the defenders of Oporto were completely cut off from the world. Food became so scarce that even in the army and in the hospitals rations were reduced to a minimum allotment of rice and codfish.

The city's fuel reserves also were completely exhausted, and in order to cook their food, seasoned with sugar or chocolate in place of salt, the inhabitants had to go out into no man's land, fell trees, and drag them back to the city, bit by bit, under a rain of bullets. They would foolishly risk their lives for a few sticks of wood. When all other resources had been exhausted, the wood-work of the houses was taken to burn in the kitchen stoves. The French and English in the city organized true hunting parties with dogs and cats as the game, which they afterward ate. Many taverns and other eating places would buy these animals by the pound and put them on their respective menus.

To make matters even worse, a great many died from an epidemic of typhus and cholera that had been brought to the city in General Solignac's baggage. To complete this Dantesque series of afflictions, the destructive and implacable bombardment kept up incessantly. In the beginning the Santo-Ildefonso quarter, which was sheltered by Mount Pilar, and that of Cedofeita were more or less safe from the cannonading; but after February the royalists, by amplifying the range of their batteries, succeeded in bringing these districts also under fire. On February 14th there were ten days' rations on hand and eighty cartridges per man. From the arsenal soldiers carried pails and barrels of sand to the batteries, pretending that it was gunpowder, in order that the public might not become alarmed and panicky. In view of all this (the *Evening Mail* even carried the news that Oporto had surrendered and Dom Pedro had fled), the British consul offered his good offices in coming to terms with Dom Miguel; but Pedro energetically declined: "Never will I do a thing like that." On the 18th the brave boatmen of the Douro, under an extremely heavy fire from both banks as they struggled against the raging waters, managed to land a small stock of munitions and supplies. On the 22nd arrangements were made with an English merchant for the purchase of three thousand hundredweight of codfish. Once again the city had been saved.

CHAPTER FOURTEEN

VICTORY AT LAST

While Oporto's defenders were fighting desperately, one of the cleverest of Dom Pedro's agents was busy in London, his mission being to procure money, ships, officers, soldiers, horses, and war equipment. A most capable diplomat and former minister of John VI, who had made him a marquis, a friend of the outstanding personalities of his age such as Alfieri, Schlegel, Sismondi, the two Humboldts, Gay Lussac, Benjamin Constant, and Madame de Staël, Palmela was possessed of a brilliant mind and had embraced the liberal cause with sincerity and an understanding of the historical moment in which he was living. As Portuguese ambassador to London, he had tendered his resignation immediately after the Miguelist coup and had thereupon found himself the virtual leader and center of Dona Maria II's party in Europe. His antecedents and the high respect he enjoyed in the various courts of Europe by reason of his moderate opinions had a great deal to do with tempering the suspicious attitude of nearly all the governments toward the revolutionary extremism of most of the emigrees.

Inasmuch as it was believed inevitable in all the capitals that Dom Pedro's expedition would fail, Palmela's financial negotiations were becoming all the while more difficult. It was true that the enemy had not succeeded in breaking through Oporto's defense lines, but time was rapidly consuming the mainstay of liberal resistance, that is to say: money. Money with which to maintain the fleet and foreign battalions and pay off the soldiers. The governments of Paris and London having definitely refused to aid him and it being impossible for him to have recourse to the bankers so long as the amortization on the old loans was unpaid, Palmela resolved to turn to individual citizens, to the British people themselves, and proceeded to address a pathetic appeal to them in Dom Pedro's name. This worked a true miracle, and in less than four days the subscription lists had mounted to £80,000. Such was the enthusiasm that liberal ideas evoked. With this money Palmela was able to employ the services of a sailor possessed of real genius—his name was Napier—and went on to organize the famous "steamboat expedition." On the 28th of May, 1833, he left London on the *City of Walesford*, followed by a number of ships laden with soldiers and bound for the city that was suffering so greatly.

The arrival of these reinforcements made it possible for Dom Pedro to take the offensive. The first operation was to consist in the landing of a strong column in the southern provinces by way of distracting the royalist troops and compelling them to fight on two fronts. The command of the expedition was entrusted to the count of Vila-Flor, whose bravery and devotion Pedro had rewarded by conferring upon him the title of Duke of Terceira. Preoccupied with the defense of Lisbon, Cadaval and the Count of Basto, Miguel's lieutenants, had left Algarve practically without a garrison, and the Viscount of Molelos did not have more than 1,600 men with which to defend that province. The latter general, nevertheless, rapidly concentrated at the Almargem bridge the three royalist divisions and a detachment of cavalry in order to meet the liberal attack. Terceira easily drove him back and continued on his march. On the 26th

he was in Olhão and on the following day he made a triumphal
entry into Faro. Arriving by sea, Palmela set up a civil government and proclaimed the queen. On the 28th two of Dom Pedro's
brigades made a sally, one upon Loulé and the other upon
Quarteira, where they met and continued in pursuit of the enemy,
who now retired to Santa Clara and from there to Messejana. In
a week's time the whole of Algarve had been occupied.

It was then that the Lisbon government committed a very
grave mistake. In place of keeping its fleet upon the Tagus, in
order to assure the safety of the capital, it sent the ships out to
give battle, which was precisely what the commander of the
liberal fleet desired.

Napier was a curious type. The historian Soriano has given
us a picture of him:

A man of ordinary stature, somewhat corpulent, with a round
face and with a black silk handkerchief under his beard and attached to his head as if he had the toothache; a large, round,
broad-brimmed hat of the kind the Quakers wear; wide blue
trousers, white shoes and stockings, and a navy officer's greatcoat
—such was the appearance of this outstanding military personage
as we saw him for the first time.

On the morning of the 3rd of July, in the midst of a fearful
storm, the two fleets sighted each other off Cape Saint Vincent;
but owing to the high seas, they were compelled to survey each
other from afar for the course of an entire day. On the royalist
side, under the command of Aboim, there were the ships *John
VI* and *Queen;* the frigates *Martim de Freitas* and *Royal Princess;*
and the corvettes *Cybele, Isabel-Maria,* and *Royal Princess;* in
addition to two brigs and a xebec. There were ten boats in all,
354 pieces of artillery, and 3,350 men. Something like a mile and
a half to leeward was Napier's little armada consisting of the

frigates *Dom Pedro, Queen of Portugal*, and *Dona Maria II* and
the brigs *Portuense* and *Vila-Flor*, carrying in all 176 guns.
Night fell and the fleets still lay silent at a distance of less than
a rifle shot one from the other. No halfway measures, Napier
told himself; either he must gain everything or lose everything;
a partial action would do no more than prolong the queen's cause
for a few weeks; only a great and momentous victory could save
that cause.

He realized that owing to the low morale and prolonged state
of apathy of the royalist crews, a sudden bold gesture might
work miracles, and so he proceeded to draw up his plan, which
was to avoid an artillery duel, bring his five ships close up, and
board the enemy. The three frigates were to attack the *Queen*
and the *Royal Princess,* while the brigs *Portuense* and *Vila-Flor*
gave battle to the *Martim de Freitas* without being concerned
with what the three enemy corvettes, their two brigs, and the
large ship *John VI* might be doing. On the morning of the 5th,
as the sun came up, the sea was fairly calm, the wind having
dropped. By midday a fresh breeze had arisen which put Napier's
fleet to windward of the enemy, and at two o'clock he went into
battle. The royalist fleet was drawn up in close formation, pro-
ceeding under very little sail. The two large boats came first, with
the two frigates at their stern, followed at intervals by the three
corvettes and the two brigs a little to leeward.

Taking advantage of the stiff breeze that bore him down upon
the enemy, Napier gave the signal for combat. Having let down
their small boats to clear the decks, the ships lined up and rapidly
advanced, flying from their mainmasts the colors of the young
queen of Portugal. As they came within musket shot, they were
greeted by a heavy round of artillery that swept their quarter-
decks and damaged their rigging, but Napier none the less kept
on, resolutely, in the direction of the *Queen,* followed by the

frigate *Dom Pedro* and replying to the fire of the enemy's ships as he passed them. Before the *John VI* was able to attack him, he had set his rudder to windward, almost scraping the *Queen's* poop with his lateen yard. Then throwing out the grappling irons and reeling in his sails, he was able to get a firm hold on the opposing craft after having fired at close range the small guns in the prow, which were loaded almost to the brim with cannon balls and grapeshot.

Napier and his officers were the first to leap aboard the vessel, whose crew was at once swept from the deck. Barreiros, the commander, led a valiant resistance and died fighting like a lion. Some minutes later, after the decks had been swept clean, they hoisted the constitutionalist flag, and then the admiral turned his attention to the *John VI,* which, threatened at the same time by the frigate *Dom Pedro,* struck its colors without firing a shot. While this was going on, the *Dona Maria II* had taken and boarded the frigate *Royal Princess,* after having fired a few rounds at her, and the two brigs had inflicted severe damage upon the *Martim de Freitas.* Leaving the frigate *Dom Pedro* in charge of the *John VI,* Napier likewise bore down upon the *Martim de Freitas,* whose commander, Manuel Pedro de Carvalho, fought so bravely before surrendering that the admiral that very night not only offered to give him back his sword but tendered him the command of the *Queen* as well.

By six o'clock that evening the firing had completely ceased, the liberals having taken prisoner the two enemy ships of the line and two frigates, besides the corvette *Royal Princess,* which surrendered later. The only craft to escape were two of the corvettes, which made for Lisbon, and the two brigs, one of which afterward came over to the victors while the other put in at Madeira. The Miguelist fleet having been destroyed, the gateway to Lisbon was now open. Victory was merely a question of time.

Thrilled by the events of July 5th, the Duke of Terceira assembled his regiments and gave the order: "On to Lisbon!" The
large reinforcements that had been sent to Molelos, the garrison
of fifteen thousand men that defended the capital, and difficulties
of every sort that might spring up in his path—none of these
things mattered. Napier with an insignificant force had taken
prisoner a powerful fleet. Why should not he be able to repeat
the exploit on land? And so he embarked upon the adventure.
By the 13th of July he had already passed São-Bartolomeu-de-
Messines and on the 15th he entered Garvão. Molelos, in place
of taking up a position between Terceira's army and Lisbon and
offering battle to the liberals, now set out for Beja, leaving the
road to the capital entirely free. The reason for this was that a
guerrilla force had entered Beja and a letter from Bernardo de
Sá had been intercepted, recommending that the place be occupied by the liberals. Thinking to anticipate Terceira, Molelos
wasted three precious days in Beja, while the Duke continued his
onward march to the capital. Discovering his mistake, he then
set out in pursuit of the 1,500 men that made up the liberal
column.

But Terceira was going like the wind. On the 22nd he was in
Setúbal, where he defeated a small Miguelist force, and on the
following day he was within sight of Almada. From Lisbon,
Teles Jordão set out to encounter him with a division of three
thousand infantrymen and three squadrons of cavalry. There was
not a moment to be lost. In order not to be caught between two
lines of fire, it was necessary to defeat Teles Jordão as quickly as
possible and then turn upon Molelos, who was approaching by
forced marches. Terceira did not hesitate but impetuously hurled
himself upon his adversaries, obliging them to beat a retreat to
the banks of the Tagus. He pursued them on the gallop and
caught up with them in a state of great confusion in Cacilhas.

The disaster for the Miguelists was complete. Many threw themselves into the river, a countless number surrendered, and Teles Jordão lay dead. In Almada, shortly afterward, the two-colored banner was raised, an event that caused the greatest sensation in Lisbon.

Cadaval hastily called a meeting of the council. Peso-da-Régua proposed that the capital be abandoned immediately. The fortifications on the left bank of the Tagus having been captured, Napier might come up at any moment and bombard the city. What was more, the state of mind of the inhabitants did not inspire the least confidence. His plan was accepted, and at dawn the next day, under pretext of a review in the Campo Grande, Cadaval assembled his troops, consisting of twelve thousand men, and departed for Coimbra, followed by a multitude of the nobility, the clergy, and public functionaries.

The liberal revolution began in Lisbon in a most curious manner. On the morning of the 24th of July, a lively altercation occurred between some boatmen on the Sodré wharf. A passerby, a simple man of the people, took a hand in their quarrel and succeeded in calming them. And then suddenly, without anyone's expecting it, with all the strength of his lungs he let out a cry that froze the bystanders: "Long live Dona Maria II! Long live the constitutional charter!" When their first astonishment was over, many of those present began applauding with great enthusiasm the daring displayed by this unknown individual. Curious ones began coming up from all sides, and the demonstration rapidly took on the character of a popular uprising. The rebellion then spread to Corpo-Santo Square, and from there to Pelourinho and to Terreiro-do-Paço. Thoroughly terrified, the Miguelists did not offer the least resistance as mobs ran to the jails and released thousands of liberal prisoners. The blue and white banner was then raised over the fortress of St. George and weapons from the arsenal were distributed to the insurgents. The city had been conquered.

Later investigation revealed the identity of the one who had touched off this revolution. His name was Antônio Joaquim Govêrno. Merely by a couple of shouts, he had won for himself a place in history.

Despite the loss of his fleet and of the capital, Dom Miguel's position was still a strong one. Defended only by Terceira's 1,600 men plus the prisoners of Cacilhas and a few nationalist battalions, Lisbon was quite vulnerable. Algarve was swarming with guerrillas; and while Faro, Olhão and Lagos were garrisoned, they were isolated points in enemy territory. Alemtejo was once more under Miguelist rule, and the towns to the south of the Tagus might readily be taken away from the constitutionalists by any force that was sent there. As for the rest of the country, it was still looking with distrust upon the liberal invaders and pro-testing its loyalty to the absolute monarch. The royalists had not lost strength. What they had lost was their spirit; but in this war spirit was to prove to be of greater worth than armed might.

The arrival of the Marshal Louis de Bourmont and his brother officers, veterans of the Vendée, was looked upon by the Miguel-ists as a circumstance that offset the liberal successes in the south. Bourmont, famous for his conquest of Algiers, had been one of those responsible for the disaster of Waterloo. As a result of his treason—he had gone over to the enemy with a group of officers and with copies of Napoleon's plans—the emperor had not been able wholly to crush Blücher's Prussians at Ligny, as he had counted upon doing. Three days later, when Wellington's squadron might have been wiped out once and for all, an infernal cannonading had burst upon the Napoleonic right: it was Blücher reappearing to transform the face of the world.

Upon assuming the high command of Miguel's troops, Bour-

mont declared on the night of July 24th that they would dine in
Oporto the next day. This they did not do. After nine hours of
the most strenuous fighting, the marshal was forced to retire,
having lost more than four thousand men. The spell had been
undone.

At a phase of the war in which minutes were precious, the
new royalist generalissimo spent long days in observing the
Oporto lines without knowing whether to attack them again or
hasten to the defense of the capital. Summoning his various
military advisers, he leisurely studied the advantages and dis-
advantages of both plans. He finally decided upon the latter one
but was not able to carry it out. In place of going on to Lisbon as
fast as he could in order not to give Dom Pedro time to gain new
recruits and fortify the city, he continued to consult with his
generals and deploy his troops in futile movements. On the 2nd
day of August he withdrew his artillery from the fortresses of
Castro, Ervilha, and Serralves, but not until the 6th did he begin
his slow retreat to Coimbra. There he remained, elaborating fresh
plans until the 18th. Meanwhile, Dom Pedro was expending his
efforts in throwing up defense lines for the capital with that energy
and singleness of devotion of which only he was capable. "There
were days," a witness tells us, "when daybreak found him among
the laborers on the fortifications and when he did not return to
the palace until sundown."

Finally, on the 18th of August, the royalists once more began
their march upon the capital. There were three columns in all,
the first of which, commanded by La Rochejacquelein, was to
occupy Salvaterra-de-Magos in order to assure communications
with Alemtejo; while the second was to proceed in the direction
of Santarem; and the third, led by Bourmont and Dom Miguel
himself, was to march toward Leria as a reserve force. The delay,

however, was to prove fatal for them. They were to find Lisbon transformed into an all but impregnable citadel. "The fortifications, distributed in a semicircle, crowned the heights from Xabregas to Alcântara, with 184 cannon. In this manner both banks of the Tagus were protected; and on the river were the warships, lined up from Junqueira to Belem and from Beato to Vila-Franca."

This control of the sea made possible the rapid movement of troops from Oporto to Lisbon or any other point along the seaboard, which was a considerable advantage. As for the recruiting of personnel, that too was proving effective, and before the end of September there were already 18,752 fighters in the front lines. Bourmont's procrastination had made it possible for Lisbon to be reinforced with an additional cavalry regiment, three infantry corps, and twenty militia battalions, mobile and stationary. In Leiria the French marshal and conqueror of Algiers spent a few days more fitting out the infantry and organizing a flying column for reconnoitering purposes; and he lost still more time at Caldas in an effort to get in communication with the other columns on his left.

The first assault did not come until daybreak of the 5th of September. The Miguelists advanced with a force of from ten thousand to twelve thousand men divided into six columns supported by eight pieces of artillery and strong cavalry detachments. The assault was a violent one until afternoon, but the city put up a gallant resistance and the enemy was compelled to fall back. In the course of the action the Duke of Terceira was wounded and had his horse shot from under him, and Dom Pedro himself, quite heedless of the heavy rifle fire, almost lost his life while working near the embrasure of a cannon in the redoubt of Cova-da-Onça. On the following day the liberals waited for a fresh attack that did not come; for the royalists had returned to the method of the siege and sought to close their lines all the way from Alto-de-Monsanto to Portela. This was in vain, however, for the city could be easily supplied with provisions from the south and by way of the Tagus. The only result was that Dom Pedro and his aides were able peacefully to continue their work of fortifying the town by correcting those defects they had discovered in the course of the first attack, thereby rendering the place harder to take than ever.

Seeing that they had already lost their prestige, Bourmont and his officers then prepared for the 14th of September an "infallible" night attack; but this failed like the first one, and the star that had shone with so much luster upon the battlefields of North Africa was dimmed from that day forth. Bourmont's successor, the Scotch general MacDonell, thereupon assumed the task of taking the city. He spent many days in preparation and fixed upon the 11th of October for the grand assault; but on the evening of the 10th he met with the most disconcerting of surprises when he himself was violently attacked by the liberal troops. Being forced to lift the siege, he retired to Santarem without having succeeded in carrying out the plans he had so carefully elaborated. It was only Dom Miguel's coolness and the cleverness of the new commander that saved the troops from being entirely destroyed; and despite the severe punishment inflicted on the center and the left, the retreat was technically a perfect one.

The Miguelists did indeed lack that courage of which the liberals had so much and to spare. With a little audacity, they might have turned back to Lisbon after the second day's retreat when they found themselves free of pursuit by the enemy. A good night's march by the Sacavem road would have done the rest. The effect would really have been theatrical. In addition to the capital itself, they would have taken the queen, who had arrived on the 22nd of September with her entire court; and with such hostages as these victory would have been guaranteed. But they deemed it more prudent to retreat. What they lacked was the desperate tongue-lashings of Dona Carlota. The aged queen had died a short while before, overwhelmed with apprehension at seeing her life's dream collapse as the plague of liberalism spread over the country. In her the absolutists lost their most powerful bulwark. Brave and handsome but without the gift of command, Dom Miguel felt unprotected. He now had to depend upon his own resources in confronting his brother; and he still remembered those battles they had fought as youngsters in the Rio suburbs, at the head of their youthful "armies"—he had been the one who always lost. He had thought that this war would afford him a revenge, but once again "big brother" was to have the better of it.

MacDonell, meanwhile, threw up splendid fortifications around Santarem and devoted himself to the task of training his army of fifteen thousand men and reestablishing order and discipline. He proposed to remain there whatever happened until there appeared upon the Tagus the fleet that Dom Miguel's agents were purchasing in England with money from the treasury of Dona Carlota Joaquina. Then he would resume the offensive. Grave misunderstandings, however, had arisen between him and some of Dom Miguel's aides, and he found that there was nothing for him to do but to demand that they resign or tender his own resignation. Ill advised in the matter, Miguel preferred to let him go, and replaced him with Póvoas, who was old, tired, and overly prudent.

On the 15th of January, Saldanha, who had already succeeded in lifting the siege of Oporto, went on to take Leiria, which was the first step toward isolating Santarem. He then advanced upon Torres-Novas, where he hurled the queen's lancers against Chaves's famous cavalry and dispersed it. Póvoas sent five thousand men to Pernes to cut off Saldanha's rear, but the latter general, suspecting this plan, also marched on Pernes and in a surprise attack annihilated more than half of the royalist division. Some days later the bloody battle that took place in the narrow gorge of Almoster, where Saldanha had succeeded in luring the enemy by pretending to retreat, spelled the end of the royalist cause.

The battle of Asseiceira was the *coup de grâce*. In addition to their dead and wounded, the Miguelists lost more than 1,400 prisoners, including 64 officers, along with four flags, and all their artillery, munitions, and supplies. Surrounded on all sides, Santarem could hold out no longer, since it had nothing left to depend upon but the narrow corridor to Alemtejo. Silent and downcast, the royalists began their exodus, crossing the Tagus and marching in the direction of Montemor-o-Novo. Sharing in their defeat, Dom Miguel went up and down the river giving orders and helping all by his presence and the strength of his arm. Entering Santarem on the 18th of May, the liberals caught up with the rearguard of the enemy, which was trying to gain the left bank of the Tagus. There was sharp rifle fire on both sides, but these were the last hostilities of the civil war.

Shut up in Evora, the Miguelists had no recourse but to surrender. "To yield was not dishonor; to have held out would have been madness." On the 26th of May the Convention of Evora-Monte was signed. Though he had it in his power to impose the harshest of conditions, Dom Pedro showed himself in victory to be endowed with a generosity that does him eternal honor. Dom Miguel was to be free to dispose of his personal property as he liked and was assured an annual pension of sixty contos.* He was given fifteen days in which to leave the country, with the

* Approximately $150,000.

understanding that he was never to return to the Peninsula or to his Portuguese dominions nor do anything to disturb the tranquillity of the kingdom, under pain of losing his right to the stipulated pension and being subject to such other consequences as his behavior might entail. A general amnesty was also granted for all political crimes, and the individuals involved, whether nationals or foreigners, were to be permitted to leave the country or to remain, as they chose. The men in the ranks were to return to their respective homes while the officers were assured of retaining their posts.

In the course of the journey to Sines, it was necessary to employ force in order to keep the excited mob from attacking Dom Miguel and slaying him. At the port where the frigate *Stag* was awaiting him, he was rudely insulted by the infuriated people who cried out for his death as they raised their clenched fists in the air and showered stones upon him. A few months before, these same ones had knelt to adore him and had placed his portrait on their altars.

How formidable is the inconstancy of the people!

CHAPTER FIFTEEN

IN DON QUIXOTE'S CHAMBER

The cannon of the civil war having been silenced, hatreds and maledictions burst forth. Vengeance! Vengeance! was the cry that went up all over the land from north to south, sowing terror among the Miguelists. In the midst of all these unleashed passions, Dom Pedro alone preserved his serenity. He alone vainly raised his voice to call for a little tolerance for the vanquished.

The siege of Oporto had irremediably undermined his health, and so many hardships and heavy cares had reduced him to a human wreck. At the age of thirty-six, this muscular man of action, the tamer of wild horses, was an impressive ruin; only his eyes held something of their old-time glow and brilliancy. The excesses of the liberals grieved him to the heart. They would have made of him his brother's executioner, an avenging arm, but he refused. He had not come to Portugal to rear scaffolds but to institute a regime of liberty and justice.

On May 27, 1834, when the magnanimous terms of Evora-Monte became known, there were noisy demonstrations, and the mob in its indignation even went so far as to hurl mud and stones at his carriage. In the theater of São-Carlos that night, there was an atmosphere of mutiny as Dom Pedro came in. Printed copies of the Convention were circulating through the audience, together with subversive manifestoes, and the troops refused to put down the disorder; but Pedro did not hesitate. Entering the theater, he calmly appeared in the front of the royal box, and at once there was a tremendous stamping of feet, accompanied by fierce cries of revolt and hoots and hisses directed at the great idol of the day before.

Dom Pedro turned pale and felt his weak legs failing under him. He raised a hand to his throat as if to repress an attack of hollow coughing but was unable to do so. There was a spurt of blood from his mouth, drenching his white handkerchief. This was the final insult—for him a death sentence. They all gazed at him, and as if by enchantment the stamping ceased and a heavy silence fell upon the theater. The instruments in the orchestra were silent and the musicians, mute with astonishment, did not know what to do. With an effort Dom Pedro bent over to the conductor and managed to say to him in a hoarse voice:

"You may begin."

And the show went on.

From that night, his sufferings grew worse. A medical bulletin of July, 1834, stated: "His Imperial Majesty, the Duke of Braganza, after nine months of grave and obstinate illness, has now fortunately been almost completely restored to health." But this was not true. He was on the edge of the grave. The disease was avidly devouring his lungs. Before he died, however, he wished to visit Oporto as he had promised; and the enthusiasm and the affectionate demonstrations that he met with on the part of his sympathizers in that city moved him profoundly.

"There!" he murmured to Dona Amelia. "Was I right or not? Are not these my own loyal *Portuenses?*"

The fatigue occasioned by this journey shortened his days still further. Returning to Queluz, he was not able to rest as much as he should, for on the 14th of August he had to go to Lisbon to preside over the opening of the Cortes. Mounting the tall stairway of São-Bento was extremely painful for him. At every step he had to stop and pant. It seemed he would never reach the top. The address from the throne was a long one, relating all the things that had happened since the death of John VI, and it left him exhausted. The administering of the oath of regent on the 30th of August of necessity took place in one of the halls at Ajuda, since it was impossible for him to make another appearance at São-Bento.

Growing weaker all the time and feeling his life slowly ebbing away, he dictated his will on the 15th of September. His children, legitimate and bastard, all became brothers and sisters in a last expression of his desires. No offspring of his impulses or his loves was left unprovided for in the clauses of this document. He enumerated them one by one with a thoughtfulness stimulated by a world of memories. He wanted his funeral to be that of a mere general. He had been emperor and king, but it was enough for him to end his days as a soldier who had done his duty. On the following day he signed other important papers, and on the 17th, calmly and with resignation, received the rites of the Church.

On the 18th he sent word to the Chamber: "The state of my health . . . prohibits me from taking cognizance of public affairs, and in these circumstances I request you to provide the proper remedy. My most ardent prayers go up to heaven for the public welfare." The response of the Congress was immediate and took the form of a declaration of the queen's majority. Lovingly, Maria da Gloria then came up to the bedside of her dying father and placed upon his bosom the Grand Cross of the Most Noble Order of the Tower and Sword, as a recognition of valor, loyalty, and merit. It was her first act as reigning sovereign. Dom Pedro gave a faint, sad smile, and Dona Amelia stifled a sob. This was an epic moment: a modern Dulcinea rewarding her wounded hero, her knight errant. Upon the walls the scenes from Cervantes took on new meaning.

On the 19th he sent for his aides-de-camp and ordered them to bring him a soldier of the Fifth Chasseurs. That was Terceira's battalion, nucleus of the liberating army that in the course of five years of struggle had covered itself with glory. Tremulous with emotion, the soldier hesitantly drew near. As he pressed the man to his panting bosom, Dom Pedro said to him: "Transmit to your comrades this last embrace of mine." And then this hero from the ranks, who had won the medal of the Tower and Sword for acts of bravery, a veteran of the early days of the campaign and of the siege of Oporto, cried like a child. "He appeared to be nailed to the floor, without the power to move. It was necessary to take him by the hand and lead him off as if he had been a blind man." The next day Dom Pedro once more received the sacraments and embraced the crucifix as he felt the end drawing near, slowly, implacably. His wife's tenderness and affection did not fail him for an instant. Overcome with grief, she languished at his side. His life was failing fast; it was but a flickering candle now, soon to go out.

"Darling Amelia," he contrived to stammer, as a last flash lighted up his all but lifeless eyes, "when my heart is taken from my bosom, send it to the city of Oporto. I bequeath it as an eternal symbol of my gratitude to that city's loyal sons."

At two-thirty in the afternoon on September 24th, even as the sun was gilding the fields around Queluz, the eyes of the soldier king gleamed for one last time, and his white hands, exuding a cold sweat, with a supreme effort were raised to grope for his wife and daughter.

Queluz had been his cradle, and Queluz was his grave. Destiny would have it that this extraordinary man, after a stormy and romantic life, should close his eyes on the exact spot on which he had first opened them some three decades before. There, in the so-called "Don Quixote Chamber," at one of the extremities of the palace, beside that same stone stair leading down to the garden, beside the same oratory with the austere lines, looking up at the very same pictures of the Knight of the Mournful Countenance—it was there he died.

Through all the realm there echoed the lament of the poet Herculano:

> Plant the acacia, symbol of the free,
>   Beside the ashes of the brave:
> He was a king, 'gainst tyrants fought—
>   Weep, weep for him, now in his grave.

NOTES

CHAPTER ONE
  [1] Raul Brandão, *El Rey Junot*, p. 83.
  [2] *Op. cit.*, p. 35.
  [3] *Op. cit.*, p. 108.

CHAPTER TWO
  [1] Luiz Edmundo, *A Corte de D. João no Rio de Janeiro*, pp. 710, 711.
  [2] *Op. cit.*
  [3] Pedro Calmon, *O Rei do Brasil*, p. 229.

CHAPTER THREE
  [1] Alberto Rangel, *D. Pedro e a Marquesa de Santos*, p. 15.
  [2] *Ibid.*
  [3] Pedro Calmon, *O Rei do Brasil*, p. 20.
  [4] Alberto Rangel, *op. cit.*, p. 24.

CHAPTER FOUR
  [1] Tobias Monteiro, *Historia do Império—A Elaboração da Independência*, p. 176.
  [2] *Ibid.*, pp. 178–180.
  [3] *Ibid.*, p. 172.

CHAPTER SIX
  [1] Tobias Monteiro, *Historia do Império*, p. 372.
  [2] Alberto Rangel, *D. Pedro e a Marquesa de Santos*, p. 34.
  [3] *Ibid.*
  [4] *As Quatro Coroas de Pedro I*, Sérgio Corrêa da Costa (Rio, 1941).

CHAPTER SEVEN
[1] Tobias Monteiro, *Historia do Império.*
[2] *Ibid.*
[3] *Ibid.*
[4] *Ibid.*
[5] Alberto Rangel, *D. Pedro e a Marquesa de Santos,* pp. 27, 28.
[6] *Ibid.,* pp. 324, 325.

CHAPTER EIGHT
[1] Alberto Rangel, *D. Pedro e a Marquesa de Santos,* p. 132.
[2] *Ibid.,* p. 126.
[3] *Ibid.,* p. 139.
[4] Pedro Calmon, *Brasil e América,* p. 40.
[5] Alberto Rangel, *op. cit.,* p. 218.

CHAPTER NINE
[1] Alberto Rangel, *D. Pedro e a Marquesa de Santos,* p. 185.
[2] *Ibid.,* p. 181.

CHAPTER ELEVEN
[1] Alberto Rangel, *D. Pedro e a Marquesa de Santos,* pp. 236, 237.
[2] *Ibid.,* p. 296.

CHAPTER TWELVE
[1] Pedro Calmon, *O Rei Cavaleiro,* p. 256.
[2] F. Pereira de Magalhães, *Apontamentos para a História Diplomática de Portugal,* pp. 94, 95.
[3] Oliveira Martins, *Portugal Contemporâneo,* Vol. I, pp. 299, 300.

BIBLIOGRAPHY

Aguiar, Antonio Augusto de, *Vida do Marquês de Barbacena*. Imprensa Nacional, Rio, 1896.

Brandão, Raul, *El Rey Junot*.

Calmon, Pedro, *O Rei Cavaleiro*. Com. Edit. Nacional, S. Paulo, 1933.

———, *O Rei do Brasil*. José Olympio, Rio, 1935.

———, *Brasil e América*. José Olympio, Rio, 1943.

Calogeras, Pandiá, *Formação Histórica do Brasil*, 3rd ed. Com. Edit. Nacional, S. Paulo, 1938.

Capefigue, M., *L'Europe depuis l'avénement du roi Louis-Philippe*, 10 vols. Paris, 1845–1846.

Cartas e Mais Peças Oficiais Dirigidas a S.M. o Senhor D. João VI pelo Príncipe Real o Senhor D. Pedro de Alcântara. Imprensa Nacional, Lisbon, 1822.

Carvalho, M. A. Vaz de, *Vida do Duque de Palmela*, 3 vols. Imprensa Nacional, Lisbon, 1898.

Castilho, A. Feliciano de, *Tributo Português à Memória do Libertador*. Galhardo e Irmãos, Lisbon, 1836.

Castro, J. F. Borges de, *Coleção de Tratados, Convenções, Contratos e Atos Públicos celebrados entre a coroa de Portugal e as mais potências desde 1640 até ao Presente*. Imprensa Nacional, Lisbon, 1857.

Chaby, Claudio de, *Apontamentos biográficos de S.M.I. o Sr. D. Pedro IV, Duque de Bragança*. Imprensa Nacional, Lisbon, 1864.

Conde de La Hure, *História de D. João VI*. Manuscript at the Biblioteca Nacional, Rio de Janeiro.

———, *História de D. Pedro I*. Manuscript at the same library, under n. 1–36–7–6.

Corrêa da Costa, Sérgio, *As quatro corôas de Pedro I*. Civilização Brasileira, Rio, 1941.

————, *D. Pedro I e Metternich—Traços de uma Guerra Diplomática*. A Noite Editora, Rio, 1942.

Debidour, *Histoire Diplomatique de l'Europe*. F. Alcan, Paris, 1891.

Debret, *Voyage pittoresque et historique au Brésil*. Firmin Didot Frères, Paris, 1835–1839.

Despachos e Correspondência do Duque de Palmela, 4 vols. Imprensa Nacional, Lisbon, 1851–1869.

Edmundo, Luiz, *A Corte de D. João no Rio de Janeiro*, 3 vols. Rio, 1941.

Herculano, Alexandre, *Opúsculos*, Vol. II. Lisbon, 1873.

Lima, Oliveira, *O Reconhecimento do Império*. H. Garnier, Rio, 1901.

————, *D. Pedro e D. Miguel*. Cia. Melhor, S. Paulo, 1907.

————, *D. João VI no Brasil*. Rio, 1909.

Lyra, Heitor, "Trabalho da diplomacia brasileira para casar D. Pedro I," *Rev. Americana*, November, December, 1919.

Magalhães, Felix Pereira de, *Apontamentos para a Historia Diplomática de Portugal*. Lisbon, 1871.

Marquês do Lavradio, *D. João VI e a Independência do Brasil*. Lisbon, 1937.

Marquês de Resende, *Elogio Histórico do Senhor Rei Dom Pedro IV*. Tip. da Academia, Lisbon, 1867.

————, *Eclaircissemens historiques*. Everat Imprimeur, Paris, 1832.

————, *Elogio Histórico de S.M.I. o Senhor D. Pedro, Duque de Bragança*. Lisbon, 1837.

Matos, Raymundo José de Cunha, *Memórias da Campanha do Senhor Dom Pedro de Alcântara, Ex-Imperador do Brasil, no Reino de Portugal*, 2 vols. Seignot-Plancher & Cie., Rio, 1833.

Martins, Oliveira, *História da Civilização Ibérica*. Lisbon, 1909.

————, *Portugal Contemporâneo*, 2 vols. Lisbon, 1883.

————, *História de Portugal*, 2 vols. Lisbon, 1882.

Menezes, M. J. de, *Exposição Histórica da Maçonaria no Brasil*. Rio, 1857.

Monglave, Eugène de, *Correspondance de Don Pèdre Ier*. Paris, 1827.

Monteiro, D. J. L. de Souza, *Vida de Dom Pedro IV*. Lisbon, 1836.

Monteiro, Tobias, *História do Império—A Elaboração da Independência*. F. Briguiet & Cie., Rio, 1927.

————, *História do Império—O Primeiro Reinado*. Rio, 1939.

Owen, Hugh, *The Civil War in Portugal*. London, 1836.

Pace, Carlo, *Resumo Histórico da Maçonaria no Brasil*. Rio, 1896.

Pascual, A. D. de, *Rasgos Memoraveis do Sr. D. Pedro I*. Rio, 1862.

Passos, Carlos de, *D. Pedro IV e D. Miguel I*. Porto, 1936.

Pimentel, Alberto, *A Corte de D. Pedro IV*. Porto, 1896.

Rangel, Alberto, *D. Pedro I e a Marquesa do Santos*. Tours, France, 1928.
Soriano, Luz, *História do Cerco do Porto,* 2 vols. Porto, 1889.
Varnhagen, F. A. de, *História da Independência do Brasil*. Rio, 1917.

INDEX